STUDIES IN AMERICAN LITERATURE

Volume XVI

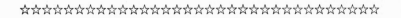

THE FICTION
OF
JOHN DOS PASSOS

by

JOHN D. BRANTLEY
Trinity University

1968
MOUTON
THE HAGUE · PARIS

LIBRARY OF CONGRESS CATALOG CARD NUMBER: 68-13347

Printed in The Netherlands by Mouton & Co., Printers, The Hague

For Jaynet

TABLE OF CONTENTS

INTRODUCTION

1

In the United States, John Dos Passos is usually omitted from lists of major modern novelists. Instead, he is most often noted as a first rate minor writer, not the most attractive of all possible distinctions. In some respects, however, the distinction is valid. Dos Passos does not have the creative imagination of Faulkner, the variety of Steinbeck, nor the high consistency of Hemingway – all his contemporaries. But Dos Passos cannot be easily dismissed: he has chronicled the social, economic, and political history of this nation from the turn of the century to the present day – certainly the project of a major rather than a minor writer. More, Dos Passos has written *Manhattan Transfer* and *U.S.A.*, both major works.

With the twentieth century American rage for simplification, critics have persistently viewed Dos Passos' works from either the purely aesthetic or the purely political point of view. The first view comes near destroying him utterly; the second makes him a saint or a demon, depending on the politics of the critic. I have avoided placing undue emphasis on either of these views or on biography, which itself is often misleading. At the same time, I have recognized Dos Passos' involvement with the events and the ideas of the times in which he has lived and which he has written about. By studying all of his works – novels, plays, poems, short stories, and non-fiction – chronologically, I have sought to bring sufficient light to the novels to make clear the evolving pattern, both in theme and in technical skills.

2

For Dos Passos, art came first, but it came hard. *One Man's Initiation-1917* (1920) is an emotional response to war, a necessary catharsis perhaps, but a weak novel. The next novel, *Three Soldiers* (1921), is also an emotional response to war, but it is cast in a well conceived although poorly executed structural frame that suggests Dos Passos' increasing concern with his art. In his art novel, *Streets of Night* (1923), Dos Passos was not using his army experiences and so was thrown upon his own resources for the first time. This explains why it is better technically but has much less content than *One Man's Initiation-1917* and why it has so much of the undergraduate ring. The novel almost has to have been conceived and begun before the author left Harvard to go to France. *Manhattan Transfer* (1925) is much too good to represent a mere two-year's improvement over *Streets of Night*: *Manhattan Transfer* is the high water mark. Dos Passos came up to it in *U.S.A.*, but he has never achieved a higher level. It represents his best effort at moulding content into an artistic form, and it is responsible for half his literary reputation.

It was during the twenties and early thirties that Dos Passos conducted his tenuous flirtation with communism and so provided the materials for politically minded critics. Perhaps the most outrageous act, from the viewpoint of "Right" minded individuals was his defense of Sacco and Vanzetti in *Facing the Chair; Story of the Americanization of Two Foreignborn Workmen*. In the same period were three plays – *Airways, Inc.*, *Fortune Heights*, and *The Garbage Man* – which constituted a sharp, if poorly written attack on the materialistic status quo. Then, in the early thirties came the three volumes of *U.S.A.*, and the political propagandist had arrived. Critics began to comb back through the early novels. They found the anarchists in *One Man's Initiation-1917* and in *Manhattan Transfer* – in the early period Dos Passos always preferred anarchists to communists – communists are not really prevalent in his books until later when they are, more often than not, the villains. The critics found rebellion everywhere, and "Right" thinking regents fired a University president because students were allowed to read *U.S.A.* But the furor was wasted; the murder of Trotsky and the dictatorial policies of Stalin had already cooled Dos Passos' ardor.

Eventually Dos Passos identified that which he was attacking in his novels. *Attacking* is used advisedly here because Dos Passos has rarely written in defense of anything; on the contrary, he has struck out in at least a dozen different directions in his literary career, attacking capitalism and communism, big business and labor, Democrats and Republicans. What he has been fighting all along, what appeared to him at first to rest only with big business but what he later saw revealed in countless other places, is power – specifically, organizational power. That power may reside in a political party, a system of government or economics, a set of social mores, or in some great impersonal force, perhaps arising from the conflict or union of two or more such organizations. In general, it may be anything outside of the individual big enough or powerful enough to have a shaping effect on the lives of men, and usually it is founded on ideals conceived for the good of men. It may or may not continue to work for those ideals, but at the moment Dos Passos attacks it as the "machine", its primary purpose has become self-perpetuation. According to Dos Passos, in novel after novel, it is at the point of self-perpetuation that the "machine" becomes impersonal, careless of the individual, and most apt to be destructive to the very ideals it was designed to achieve. In the early novels, the "machine" is large, abstract, and not clearly identified; in the later novels, the "machine" is specific, concrete, and clearly identified.

I. THE DEVELOPMENT OF THE TOOLS

1

John Dos Passos' professional literary career was inaugurated by the publication in quick succession of two war novels. The appearance of at least one such novel very early in his career was to be expected, since he was a participant in World War I. The first novel, *One Man's Initiation-1917* (1920) is a series of reactions held together by a central character. The book opens with three swift chapters which move Martin Howe, a volunteer ambulance driver, across the ocean to Bordeaux, to Paris, to the front. The remainder of the book contains a series of episodes including gas attacks by the germans, an artillery barrage which destroys a Gothic abbey containing both an aid station and an ammunition dump, a short pass to Paris, seas of mud to be negotiated in the ambulance, a political discussion with French radicals, and more gas attacks and more shelling. The book is hardly a narrative in the sense of having a beginning, a middle, and an end. Many of the episodes could be moved from one chapter to another without doing violence to the narrative, but there is a kind of thematic movement and a fairly steady show of improvement of the author's technical skill in presenting the episodes and in Martin Howe's reactions to them.

The "machine" in *One Man's Initiation-1917* is war. Although there are moments when Martin ponders on the causes of war, the basic focus is on battle. The theme is set forth primarily through Martin Howe's reaction to incidents which portray the horrors, the waste, and the brutalities of war. If Martin's reactions are at times overdrawn, it is because they are presented in a technically immature style. Dos Passos himself was undoubtedly aware of the immaturity and the need for a new basis for a later generation's understanding of the novel, because when it was reissued in 1945 under the title of *First Encounter,* he added "A Preface Twenty-Five Years Later" in which he pointed out the difference between the reactions to war that were experienced by the men of his generation and the men who fought in World War II:

> For one thing I think the brutalities of war and oppression came as less of a shock to people who grew up in the thirties than they did to Americans of my generation, raised as we were during the quiet afterglow of the nineteenth century, among comfortably situated people who were confident that industrial progress meant an improved civilization, more of the good things of life all around. ... To us, the European War of 1914-1918 seemed a horrible monstrosity, something outside of the normal order of things like an epidemic of yellow fewer in some place where yellow fever had never been heard of before.
>
> The boys who are fighting these present wars got their first ideas of the world during the depression years. From the time they first read the newspapers they drank in the brutalities of European politics with their breakfast coffee.[1]

The truth of this observation cannot be denied, but it is not the whole of the explanation for Martin Howe's tantrums; in the first place, the majority of Americans of Dos Passos' generation did not grow up in any sort of "afterglow" or among "comfortably situated people". The author's own *The 42nd Parallel* (1930) is sufficient evidence that for some people the times were cruel and had a horror and a brutality of their own. The point is that Martin Howe is not representative of the great mass of people of any nation in the first decades of the twentieth century; he is, rather, representative of that educated, intellectual, sensitive minority of which the author was a part and whose reactions to a first-hand encounter with the brutalities of war were indeed far more emotional than were the reactions of men to whom brutality and injustice were familiar spectres.

[1] John Dos Passes, "A Preface Twenty-Five Years Later", *First Encounter* (New York, Philosophical Library, 1945), pp. 7-8.

In the second place, Martin Howe's reactions were drawn by an apprentice artist who had considerably more to convey than his craftmanship could accommodate. It is this circumstance which produces such passages as the following description of the victim of an artillery barrage:

Where the middle of the man had been, where had been the curved belly and the genitals, where the thighs had joined with a strong swerving of muscles to the trunk, was a depression, a hollow pool of blood, that glinted a little in the cold diffusion of gray light from the west.[2]

There are many more such scenes – for example, the grimly ironic little narrative of the officer who has suffered a mental breakdown. A medic tells Martin, "He has an idea he ought to kill everyone he sees. ... Funny Idea." At this point a more practiced Dos Passos would have ended the episode, but the beginner's heavy hand is evident in the remark of an orderly: "He's crazy. He says that to stop the war you must kill everybody, kill everybody." [3]

The use of contrast and juxtaposition are technical skills of which Dos Passos was to become a master. In the first novel, however, these too are overdone. For example, the aid station is moved into the ground floor of an old Gothic abbey with the inevitable ammunition dump in the cellar. The Gothic architecture gives both Martin and his assistant driver, Tom Randolph, ample opportunity to compare the beauties of the past with the horrors of their present. "And you say we've progressed", Martin whispers to Tom.[4]

Later the abbey inspires Martin to dream:

... lives of saints, thoughts polished by years of quiet meditation of old divines; old romances of chivalry; tales of blood and death and

[2] John Dos Passos, *One Man's Initiation-1917* (London, George Allen & Unwin Ltd., 1920), p. 35.

[3] *Ibid.*, pp. 40-41. Since in this and in some subsequent novels, Dos Passos uses elipses in dialogue, I have arbitrarily adopted the practice of writing all of his elipses without spacing between the dots (. . .) and writing all of my elipses denoting omission of the text with spaces between the dots (. . .).

[4] *Ibid.*, p. 42.

love where the crude agony of life was seen through a dawnlike mist of gentle beauty.

"God! if there were somewhere nowadays where you could flee from all this cant of governments and this hideous reiteration of hatred, this strangling hatred . . ." he would say to himself, and see himself working in the fields, copying parchments in quaint letterings, drowsing his feverish desires to calm in the deep-throated passionate chantings of the endless offices of the Church.[5]

This passage, with its pointed contrast and its emotional outburst which takes Martin temporarily out of himself, away from his immediate environment, is typical of the whole book. When the Germans start shelling the abbey, Martin's reaction differs from Tom's because Martin blames both sides for the destruction:

"God, I hate them for that!" said Randolph between his teeth.
    "What do you want? It's an observation post."
    "I know, but damn it!" [6]

When Dos Passos follows one of his uncomfortably photographic descriptions with a light touch, the contrast is abrupt and pointed:

Martin remembers the beating legs of a mule rolling on its back on the side of the road and, steaming in the fresh morning air, the purple and yellow and red of its ripped belly.
    "Dit you get the smell of almonds? I sort of like it", says Randolph, drawing a long breath as the car slowed down again.[7]

Even when Martin goes on "permission" to Paris, the brutalities of war are never far away. They follow him in the form of a drunken Englishman who repeats over and over the story of how a wounded German prisoner was killed:

He plucked at Martin's arm, a serious set look coming suddenly over his grey eyes. "It was like this" – his breath laden with whiskey was like a halo round Martin's head – "the Hun was a nice little chap, couldn't 'a' been more than eighteen; had a shoulder broken and he thought my pal was fixing the pillow. He said 'Thank you' with a funny little German accent. . . . Mind you, he said 'Thank you'; that's what hurt. And the man laughed. God damn him, he laughed when the poor devil said 'Thank you!' And the grenade blew him to hell." [8]

[5] *Ibid.*, pp. 43-44.
[6] *Ibid.*, p. 46.
[7] *Ibid.*, pp. 74-75.
[8] *Ibid.*, p. 55.

The emotional impact of this episode is heightened by the cliché of the woman who asks Martin what the English soldier is saying. Martin answers,

"He's telling about a German atrocity."
"Oh, the dirty Germans! What things they've done" the women answered mechanically.[9]

Gradually the episodes dealing with death, destruction, and brutality become more violent and are intended to carry a greater impact. Then, in the central chapter, the whole problem of war and its effect on the individual is symbolized in an elaborate, rather overdrawn episode:

It was the fifth time that day that Martin's car had passed the cross-roads where the calvary was. Someone had propped up the fallen crucifix so that it tilted dark despairing arms against the sunset sky where the sun gleamed like a huge copper kettle lost in its own steam. The rain made bright yellowish stripes across the sky and dripped from the cracked feet of the old wooden Christ, whose gaunt, scarred figure hung out from the tilted cross, swaying a little in the beating of the rain. . . . He stared curiously at the fallen jowl and the cavernous eyes that had meant for some country sculptor ages ago the utterest agony of pain. Suddenly he noticed that where the crown of thorns had been about the forehead of the Christ someone had wound barbed wire. He smiled, and asked the swaying figure in his mind.

"And you, what do you think of it?"
For an instant he could feel wire barbs ripping through his own flesh.

A column of troops marches past the crucifix.

The faces drooped under the helmets, titled to one side or the other, distorted and wooden like the face of the figure that dangled from the cross.

One of the stragglers who floundered along through the churned mud of the road after the regular tanks had passed stopped still and looked up at the tilted cross. From the next cross-roads came, at intervals, the sharp twanging ping of shrapnel bursting.

The straggler began kicking feebly at the prop of the cross with his foot, and then dragged himself off alter the column. The cross fell forward with a dull splintering splash into the mud of the road.[10]

[9] *Ibid.*, pp. 56-57.
[10] *Ibid.*, p. 72.

After this portrayal of the barbarity of war, Martin is ready for some conclusion, some final word of either hope or despair, but the author is not. First Martin must react to war in a general way. He sees that

The woods all about him were a vast rubbish-heap; the jagged, splintered boles of leafless trees rose in every direction from heaps of brass shell-cases, of tin cans, of bits of uniform and equipment. The wind came in puffs laden with an odour as of dead rats in an attic. And this was what all the centuries of civilization had struggled for. For this had generations worn away their lives in mines and factories and forges, in fields and workshops, toiling, screwing higher and higher the tension of their minds and muscles, polishing brighter and brighter the mirror of their intelligence. For This! [11]

Soon after this generalized reaction, Martin reacts to war on a purely personal basis by feeling, for the first time, extreme fear when his aid station is shelled by the Germans. Where reaction before had been intellectual, he now reacts physically, cowering in his bunk, awaiting the inevitable arrival of death by chance. Dos Passos again introduces contrast with a short chapter describing Martin's emotions on the following morning. He looks out on an idyllic farmyard scene where a French firl is feeding chickens and ducks, and he realizes that he can't even hear the sound of the guns.

Martin's statements in Chapter IX, which contains his conversation with the French radicals, are not indicative of his acceptance of a radical creed. Although it is customary to view the book's rejection of war as political as well as aesthetic, it is doubtful that either Martin Howe or John Dos Passos was embracing anything more than a hope at that time. To be sure, he mentions hope centering upon Lenin – as well as Wilson – in the preface appended to *First Encounter,* but after twenty-five years, he remembered it as a feeling, not as a conviction, and internal evidence in his other works seems to substantiate his claim. In the preface, he says,

Looking back it is frightening to remember that naive ignorance of men and their behavior through history which enabled us to believe

[11] *Ibid.,* p. 103.

that a revolution which would throw the rascals out of the saddle would automatically, by some divine order of historical necessity, put in their places a band of benign philosophers. ... Having no knowledge of the society we had grown up in, or of the traditional attitudes that had produced in us the very ethical bent which made war and tyranny abhorrent to us, we easily fell prey to the notion that by a series of revolutions like the Russian the working people of the world could invent out of their own heads a reign of justice. ... It was this sanguine *feeling* that the future was a blank page to write on, focusing first about the speeches of Woodrow Wilson and then about the figure of Lenin, that made the end of the last war so different from the period we are now entering.[12]

Further, it should be noted that the discussions of the radicals, who range from anarchist to communist, are brought to a close without anyone's being allowed to win a convert and that although one of the men is hoarding ammunition for the revolution which he expects to take place after the war, Martin makes no offer to help in any way. He may have his hopes, but he remains uncommitted.

Martin's feelings are summed up when he tells his radical friends that Americans are "like children" who "have had no experience in international affairs" and that America is now "a military nation, an organized pirate like France and England and Germany".[13] As he enters his peroration, Martin becomes lyrical in the worst sense of the word:

"What terrifies me rather is their power to enslave our minds," Martin went on, his voice growing louder and surer as his idea carried him along. "I shall never forget the flags, the menacing exultant flags along all the streets before we went to war, the gradual unbarring of teeth, gradual lulling to sleep of people's humanity and sense by the phrases, the phrases. ... America, as you know is ruled by the press. And the press is ruled by whom? Who shall ever know what dark forces bought and bought until we should be ready to go blinded and gagged into war? ... People seem to so love to be fooled. Intellect used to mean freedom, a light struggling against darkness. Now darkness is using the light for its own purposes. ... We are slaves of bought intellect, willing slaves.[14]

[12] "A Preface Twenty-Five Years Later", pp. 8-9. Italics mine.
[13] *One Man's Initiation-1917*, p. 113.
[14] *Ibid.*, p. 114.

This is a passage of revolt against the powers that be, but it is not a passage of prophecy of a new order. It continues the theme of revulsion and carries it to a climax. As Dos Passos said in 1956,

It's hard to overestimate the revulsion wrought by the first World War in the minds of a generation that had grown up in the years of comparative freedom and comparative peace that opened the century. . . . Waste of time, waste of money, waste of lives, waste of youth. We came home with the horrors. We had to blame somebody.[15]

At the time Dos Passos was writing his first novel, the only forces he was willing to blame were the "dark" ones.

Having thus developed his theme through Martin's revulsion to sights, sounds, smells, and events and having brought Martin, through his conversation with the radicals, to an expression of antagonism for whatever "dark forces" promoted the war, Dos Passos brings the book quickly to a close. Chapter ten is a two-page chapter containing a brief episode which occurs after Martin returns to the aid station. An old man sits in the dugout carving bootstrings from the leather of the boots that have been removed from the dead and wounded. Martin buys a pair. Life goes on, and though he is repelled by it, Martin is a participant – he must have shoestrings. The last chapter, also very short, brings Martin to the side of the last of the radicals, the others having previously been killed. As he dies, the man whispers words of hope to Martin, "It's not for long. Tomorrow, the next day . . .".[16]

Although Martin Howe's reactions to the horrors of war are extreme, he has absolutely no other recourse. Since his work is that of rendering aid to others who have been caught under the wheels of the "machine", all he can do is cry out in the name of humanity as he helplessly views the destruction. In 1945 Dos Passos wrote of his first novel:

This narrative was written more than a quarter of a century ago by a bookish young man of twenty-two who had emerged half-baked from Harvard College and was continuing his education driving a ambulance behind the front in France.[17]

---

[15] John Dos Passos, *The Theme is Freedom* (New York, Dodd, Mead & Co., 1956), pp. 1-2.
[16] *One Man's Initiation-1917*, p. 128.
[17] "A Preface Twenty-Five Years Later", *First Encounter*, p. 7.

There are good and bad implications in that statement. It does explain much about his use of the primary tools of his trade: the image, the short vignette or incident, the use of irony, contrast, symbols. In virtually every case, the image, the incident, the contrast is overdone. From the standpoint of the beginning novelist, however, the main point is not that he made mistakes, but that he recognized his tools and used them, however poorly. Only one other point relative to Dos Passos' development of skills in his craft needs to be mentioned here: that is his habit of sliding from direct to indirect discourse. He uses this technique either to render more smoothly the gist of a long or rambling conversation, or to take the thought out of the colloquial language of conversation in order to state it in more emotional or – especially in some of the later novels – poetic language. For example, during a discussion between Tom Randolph and Martin Howe, such a shift occurs:

No, they had been saying, it could not go on; some day amid the rending crash of shells and whine of shrapnel fragments, people everywhere, in all uniforms, in trenches, packed in camions, in stretchers, in hospitals, crowded behind guns, involved in telephone apparatus, generals at their dinner-tables, colonels sipping liquers, majors developing photographs, would jump to their feet and burst out laughing at the solemn inanity, at the stupid, vicious pomposity of what they were doing. Laughter would untune the sky. It would be a new progress of Bacchus ... the sun would wear a broad grin and would whisper the joke to the moon, who would giggle and ripple with it all night long. . . .[18]

And that is bad writing.

2

Three Soldiers (1921) is generally recognized as Dos Passos' first real novel; certainly it reveals a broadening of scope and a more mature style. In it the theme is still more explicit than implicit, but the author's technical skills are otherwise considerably improved. The first section of the novel relates the introduction to

[18] *One Man's Initiation-1917*, pp. 52-53.

the army of Dan Fuselli and John Andrews and describes Fuselli's experiences as he goes through a Port of Embarkation and across the ocean on a troop ship. In part two, the story is continued from the viewpoint of Fuselli, relating his progress to a Medical Unit well behind the lines. Fuselli is promoted to Private First Class and is made temporary Corporal when the regular Corporal goes to the hospital. Fuselli meets Yvonne and falls in love with her, but he eventually loses her to the sergeant to whom he has introduced her. Then, when the regular Corporal comes back to the unit, Fuselli loses all hope of promotion. The unit is ordered to the front, but because he is afraid and because he has been disappointed about promotions, Fuselli wrangles a last-minute transfer to the permanent cadre of the post.

Part three is told entirely from the viewpoint of Chrisfield, whom Fuselli and Andrews meet at the training camp. Andrews is with Chrisfield through the section, but the viewpoint never shifts to him. Their unit is moved to the front soon after Fuselli's old company is moved up. Throughout the book, Chrisfield has a running quarrel with a man named Anderson, for whom he develops a deep hatred. The quarrel, entirely provoked by Chrisfield, intensifies as Anderson is gradually promoted through the ranks to sergeant. After his unit has gone into combat, Chrisfield gets lost and stumbles on the wounded Anderson, now a lieutenant, and Chrisfield kills him.

Part four begins with Andrews being wounded and going to a hospital. Although the war is over by the time he recovers, Andrews is ordered back to his division, but he applies for and gets a transfer to the student detachment at the University of Paris. He settles down to a routine of hard work on his music, a love affair with a girl named Jeanne, and an occasional evening with some sophisticated, hard-drinking friends. He encounters Fuselli, who has been put into a labor battalion. He finally stops seeing Jeanne and begins seeing Genevieve Rod, who can talk to him about music, but he foolishly goes AWOL to visit her and is caught by the Military Police who put him in a labor battalion without a trial. He deserts and goes to Paris where he meets Chris, who has deserted because he thinks that someone in the company has learned that he killed Anderson. Some of Andrew's friends try to persuade him to rejoin his detachment, but he refuses. Instead, he goes to Genevieve's country home, but she "fails" him because he is a deserter. Then his money runs out, and the Military Police capture him and take him away as the wind scatters his music manuscript around his empty room.

The structure of *Three Soldiers* is incomparably tighter and more unified than the structure of *One Man's Initiation-1917*. The structure develops in two major ways. First, the book contains the stories of three men and develops a central theme of the conflict that each has with the army. The three men are obviously representative characters: Fuselli is the lower class of San Francisco, Chrisfield is a farmboy from Indiana − "right in the middle" − and Andrews is intellectually, if not financially, of the upper class of New York city. This arrangement gives both a geographic and a cultural cross-section of the United States. It does, of course, ignore the middle class, but Dos Passos did not discover that class until he published *Chosen Country* in 1951. Using his representative men in *Three Soldiers*, Dos Passos shifts the angle of narration from the consciousness of one to another through the various sections of the book. Thus, Fuselli is used to portray the enlisted man going through induction, being a part of troop movements, and working behind the lines in time of war. Chrisfield portrays the enlisted man during training and combat. Andrews, since he is "the only one who could verbalize a moral attitude towards war",[19] is used to portray induction with Fuselli in the first section; he is present as interpreter of events with Chrisfield during most of Chrisfield's experience, and Andrews alone is used as focal point for the post-war sections. There is some structural imbalance, however; the portions related through Fuselli are almost twice the length of those related through Chrisfield, and those related through Andrews are more than twice the length of those related through Fuselli. Over half of this "war" novel, then, is devoted to action which occurs after the armistice.

[19] Blanche Housman Gelfant, *The American City Novel* (Norman, Oklahoma, University Oklahoma Press, 1954), p. 140.

One important structural element derived from the use of three distinct viewpoints is a separate climax for the narrative of each of the three men. Each of the men brings to the conflict his own inherent weakness, each is destroyed by the "machine" because of that weakness, and the denouement for each of the three is tragic to a degree proportionate to the struggle each makes with the "machine". The second major structural element is the use of metaphorical section headings which define the sections and relate them to the theme of the novel as a whole. "Making the Mould", "The Metal Cools", "Machines", "Rust", "The World Outside", and "Under the Wheels" express insistently the machine-like quality of the army and the uniformity required of the men in it. Fuselli is the point of view for most of the first two sections, Chrisfield for the third, and Andrews for almost all of the last three. To underline the metaphor of the section headings, Dos Passos often has a character express an idea which reiterates the metaphor of that section.

In this "war novel" of few battle scenes, combat is scarcely touched upon, the effects of combat upon men is not given much more treatment, and the horrors of war, so prominent in *One Man's Initiation-1917*, are almost totally absent. The war itself is ominously present in the background, but even in Chrisfield's section, violence and death never come very near; Andrews is wounded by shrapnel in the most impersonal of all possible ways. But the army, a vast and powerful "machine", is everpresent; it intrudes constantly into the minutest details of the lives of the characters and absorbs most of their thoughts. The army is the antagonist, the "machine" in the lives of the three men. It is the destroyer of liberty, individuality, and initiative; it operates on the lives of the men through its regulations which are as certain as the laws of nature and through its officers and non-commissioned officers who are as unbending as the regulations they must obey.

Fuselli is the first of a series of characters created by Dos Passos who try to live with or to join the "machine" and who are nevertheless destroyed. Such characters are ingratiating but likeable and are eager to gain advancement and security. The broad outlines of Fuselli's character are sketched by Dos Passos in the following passage:

Fuselli wrapped the blanket round his head and prepared to sleep. Snuggled down into the blankets on the narrow cot, he felt sheltered from the Sergeant's thundering voice and from the cold glare of officers' eyes. He felt cosy and happy like he had felt in bed at home, when he had been a little kid. . . . He must remember to smile at the sergeant when he passed him off duty. Somebody had said there'd be promotions soon. Oh, he wanted so hard to be promoted. . . . He must be careful not to do anything that would get him in wrong with anybody. He must never miss an opportunity to show them what a clever kid he was. "Oh, when we're ordered overseas, I'll show them," he thought ardently, and picturing to himself long movie reels of heroism he went off to sleep.[20]

The same image of Fuselli is shown over and over again. For example, when he sees the non-commissioned officers eating better food than the other enlisted men, he reacts in the same way:

"I got to get busy," he said to himself earnestly. Overseas, under fire, he'd have a chance to show what he was worth; and he pictured himself heroically carrying a wounded captain back to a dressing tent, pursued by fierce whiskered men with spiked helmets like firemen's helmets.[21]

Overseas, however, the possibilities for glorious heroism begin to take on a fearful aspect for Fuselli. He sees a man who has returned from the front suffering from an emotional breakdown, and he feels terror for the first time because the man doesn't match his Hollywood-inspired picture of the "jolly soldiers in khaki marching into towns, pursuing terrified Huns across potato fields, saving Belgian milk-maids against picturesque backgrounds".[22] Fuselli's fear is multiplied when the combat veteran remarks that medical corpsmen "didn't last long at the Chateau".[23]

Fuselli's first real temptation to rebellion against the machine comes when he is assigned to be an orderly one day for an officer.

[20] John Dos Possos, *Three Soldiers* (New York, The Modern Library, 1932), p. 11.
[21] *Ibid.*, p. 38.
[22] *Ibid.*, p. 57.
[23] *Ibid.*, p. 59.

He rebels at the thought of doing "servant's" work and being a "slavey" for an officer, yet when he notices that the corporal looks sick, he doesn't say anything. The climax of his narrative occurs when he goes to the place where he regularly meets his girl only to find the sergeant there ahead of him. It is the kind of situation into which Dos Passos frequently thrusts his characters. Fuselli must choose between standing up for his rights against the representative of the "machine" and submitting to the dictates of the machine in hopes of receiving a reward. In either case, the man faced with such a choice is, in the mind of Dos Passos, doomed. It is a matter of choosing how one will be defeated. Fuselli's defeat is recorded as follows:

Fuselli stood still with fists clenched. The blood flamed through his head making his scalp tingle.

Still the top sergeant was the top sergeant, came the thought. It would never do to get in wrong with him.[24]

For the sake of security and the hope of a permanent corporalcy, Fuselli gives up the girl he wants to marry, thus becoming a victim of the destructive effects of the "machine'. The first person he meets when he returns to the barracks that night is the corporal who has returned from the Hospital, and Fuselli knows that even his temporary promotion will be taken away from him.

When his company is ordered to the front, Fuselli, after all of his daydreams of heroism, secretly applies for a transfer so that he won't have to go, telling himself the while that now he has a job "where he would show what he was good for".[25] Dos Passos then weaves in a sharp note of contrast by having Andrews and Chrisfield – on their way to the front – pass through the town where he is stationed. Soon after this episode, the main portion of Fuselli's denouement is completed. A man in his company refuses to obey the orders of an officer and dies of a heart attack in the barracks. Fuselli betrays the extent of his own defeat as he walks away muttering, "He's crazy".[26]

Scattered through the section of the story which is seen through

[24] *Ibid.*, pp. 114-115.
[25] *Ibid.*, p. 125.
[26] *Ibid.*, p. 40.

Chrisfield are numerous remarks, usually made by Chrisfield, which keep to the fore the general theme of the book. Typical of these remarks is the one Chrisfield makes while he is on the train headed for the front: "Hell! They keep you in this goddam car like you was a convict. ...." [27] And on another occasion, he expresses his attitude toward the Infantry: "This ain't no sort o' life for a man to be treated lahk he was a nigger." [28] But these comments merely form a backdrop of resentment against which the highly localized hatred of Chrisfield is etched. Chrisfield brings to the conflict his tragic flaw of "a bit of the devil", and when resentment of the "machine" boils up within him, he directs it as unreasoning hatred against one unoffending man. The first important event is related by Chrisfield, who tells Andrews that he threatened Anderson with a knife because "He seems to think that just because ah'm littler than him he can do anything he likes with me." [29] On another occasion,

Chrisfield felt powerless as an ox under the yoke. All he could do was work and strain and stand at attention, while that white-faced Anderson could lounge about as if he owned the earth and laugh importantly like that. ... He looked peaceful, almost happy. Chrisfield clenched his fists and felt the hatred of the other man rising stingingly within him.

"Guess Ah got a bit of the devil in me," he thought.[30]

The higher the rank of Anderson and the longer Chrisfield is in the army, the greater grows Chrisfield's resentment and the more sharply it is directed against Anderson. The unreasoning quality of Chrisfield's behavior is brought out in the scene where Anderson, now a sergeant, finds Chrisfield in the barracks during duty hours. Chrisfield sullenly explains that he is "barracks guard".

"Orders was all the companies was to go out an' not leave any guard."
"Ah!"
"We'll see about that when Sergeant Higgins comes in. Is this place tidy?"
"You say Ah'm a goddamed liar, do ye?" Chrisfield felt suddenly

[27] *Ibid.*, p. 135.
[28] *Ibid.*, p. 146.
[29] *Ibid.*, p. 24.
[30] *Ibid.*, pp. 166-167.

cool and joyous. He felt anger taking possession of him. He seemed to be standing somewhere away from himself watching himself get angry.

"This place has got to be cleaned up. . . . That damn General may come back to look over quarters," went on Anderson coolly.

"You call me a goddam liar," said Chrisfield again, putting as much insolence as he could summon into his voice. "Ah guess you doan' remember me."

"Yes, I know, you're the guy tried to run a knife into me once," said Anderson coolly, squaring his shoulders. "I guess you've learned a little discipline by this time. Anyhow you've got to clean this place up. God, they haven't even brushed the bird's nests down! Must be some company!" said Anderson with a half laugh.

"Ah ain't agoin' to neither, fur you." [31]

And so their whole conflict is built; Anderson is innocent of any offense, but as representative of the "machine", he has unwittingly become the focal point for all of Chrisfield's frustations. The one-sided conflict, then, rises swiftly through Chrisfield's first plan to kill Anderson, to the actual murder which, for Chrisfield, is the climax of his army career. Although he is promoted to corporal and plans to remain in the army indefinitely, his sense of security and well-being is of short duration, and he finally deserts because he feels sure that a sergeant in the company knows he has killed Anderson.

Chrisfield, like Fuselli, is highly reminiscent of a whole series of characters scattered through the novels of Dos Passos. The man is basically a victim of his own nature and of the "machine" of which he is a part. Chrisfield, like the others of his stamp – in later novels they are often members of the I. W. W. – is a "direct actionist" who is destroyed because he attempts to fight the "machine" or its representative.

John Andrews, too, is a character of a type frequently found in Dos Passos' novels; fortunately, the character is generally more convincing in the later novels. This type often appears as the intellectual on the scene capable of interpreting the events that take place during the course of the narrative. In his capacity as interpreter, Andrews, although he is not with Fuselli and cannot

[31] *Ibid.*, pp. 168-169.

interpret for him, and although he simply does not understand the behavior of Chrisfield, nevertheless gives the most clear-cut expression of the central theme of the novel. In the section called "Making the Mold" Dos Passos reveals Andrews' first response to the army's demand for conformity and uniformity. Shortly after he enlists, he is washing windows and a rhythm comes to him which he promptly lables "Arbeit und Rhythmus":

He tried to drive the phrase out of his mind, to bury his mind in the music of the rhythm that had come to him, that expressed the dusty boredom, the harsh constriction of warm bodies full of gestures and attitudes and aspirations into moulds, like the moulds toy soldiers are cast in.[32]

The "slavery" inherent in army discipline comes harder to Andrews than to the other men, and he decides that it is because they are from the lower half of the social "pyramid" and know nothing of the "glittering other world" in which he has always lived.[33]

They were all so alike, they seemed at moments to be but one organism. This was what he had sought when he had enlisted, he said to himself. It was in this that he would take refuge from the horror of the world that had fallen upon him. ... This was much better, to let everything go, to stamp out his maddening desire for music, to humble himself into the mud of common slavery. He was still tingling with sudden anger from the officer's voice that morning: "Sergeant, who is this man?" The officer had stared in his face as a man might stare at a piece of furniture.[34]

When he is wounded, Andrews hopes he may be discharged from the army; he remembers his life as it was "before he had become a slave among slaves", and he thinks of himself and the other wounded men as "discharged automatons, broken toys laid away in rows".[35] But while he has felt resentment and humiliation from the "slavery" he so detests, Andrews has not yet begun his conflict with the vast "machine" of which he is a part and to which he has come with a feeling of depression because of his

[32] *Ibid.*, p. 18.
[33] *Ibid.*, p. 29.
[34] *Ibid.*, p. 22.
[35] *Ibid.*, p. 214.

disgust with a world in which such a war could happen. The emotional basis for the conflict is established in an interior monologue which closely resembles Martin Howe's long speech to the French radicals:

The phrase ["make the world safe for democracy"] came to Andrews' mind amid an avalanche of popular tunes, of visions of patriotic numbers on the vaudeville stage. He remembered the great flags waving triumphantly over Fifth Avenue, and the crowds dutifully cheering. . . . he had not been driven into the army by the force of public opinion, he had not been carried away by any wave of blind confidence in the phrases of bought propagandists. He had not had the strength to live. The thought came to him of all those who, down the long tragedy of history, had given themselves smilingly for the integrity of their thoughts. He had not had the courage to move a muscle for his freedom, but he had been fairly cheerful about risking his life as a soldier, in a cause he believed useless. What right had a man to exist who was too cowardly to stand up for what he thought and felt, for his whole make-up, for everything that made him an individual apart from his fellows, and not a slave to stand cap in hand waiting for someone of stronger will to tell him how to act? [36]

Thus, in a temporary lull, Andrews reaches the state of mind and emotion which, under the proper circumstances, will result in his desertion, and when he does decide to desert, he thinks of the act in terms of joining the "defeated ones" who stood for the integrity of the individual. Most of the remaining rising action of his story deals with the intensification of his feeling and the gradual arrangement of circumstances which cause him to desert. The emotional intensification continues as he thinks, "What was the good of stopping the war if the armies continued?"[37] And his humiliation is continued in such incidents as the following:

A narrow board walk led from the main road to the door. In the middle of this walk Andrews met a captain and automatically got off into the mud and saluted.[38]

Eventually the real indignities have raised his feelings to the pitch that even the most ordinary events produce an emotional outburst

---

[36] *Ibid.*, p. 221. *Cf. One Man's Initiation-1917*, p. 114.
[37] *Ibid.*, p. 259.
[38] *Ibid.*, p. 270.

in him. For example, in order to get transferred to the school Detachment at the University of Paris, Andrews has to cajole, flatter, and intrigue to get his name added to the list. No one offers him a special affront, but because he has to so lower himself, he reacts violently:

The fury of his humiliation made tears start in his eyes. He walked away from the village down the main road, splashing carelessly through the puddless, slipping in the wet clay of the ditches. Something within him, like the voice of a wounded man swearing, was whining in his head long strings of filthy names.[39]

And again, when an M.P. tells him to button his coat and then won't allow him to loiter in front of a government office, there is a similar reaction:

Andrews flushed and walked away without turning his head. He was stinging with humiliation; an angry voice inside him kept telling him that he was a coward, that he should make some futile gesture of protest. ... Was there no outlet, no gesture of expression, would he have to go on this way day after day, swallowing the bitter gall of indignation, and every new symbol of his slavery brought to his lips? [40]

It is noteworthy that Andrews assumes that any gesture he might make is doomed to be futile; his ultimate destruction, then, is to some extent self-sought. There is irony in that this emotionally wrought young man who elects to rebel against the strictures of the "machine" has an assignment which provides the greatest opportunity for personal liberty consistent with being in the army. He does not live in a barracks on an army post, he has a privately rented room in Paris; instead of military duties, he attends classes at the University. It is from this enviable assignment that he goes A.W.O.L., leaving his dogtags, the symbols of "slavery", in his room.

Andrews is apprehended, and he is sent to a labor battalion without benefit of trial or investigation. This treatment is the ultimate cruelty that the army can impose on him, and it provides the proper circumstances for desertion; but Andrews re-

[39] *Ibid.*, p. 284.
[40] *Ibid.*, p. 370.

mains strangely docile. Indeed, his desertion is barely a matter of volition: he merely accompanies another man who deserts, and thus he still has not made a conscious choice between serving the "machine" and making his "gesture".

It is for the anticlimactic purpose of his making the conscious choice that Dos Passos takes Andrews back to Paris where he learns that he could easily slip back into his detachment because he has not been reported absent. His friends plead with him, but Andrews refuses to go back, deliberately choosing desertion. The self-destruction implicit in his choice is made clear when, instead of using the money given to him by his friends to get across the border into a neutral or unoccupied country, Andrews goes to see Genevieve Rod for whom he has never demonstrated a consuming passion.

Andrews' personal relation to his act of desertion is symbolized, perhaps too obviously, in his registering with his landlady as "John Brown" – in memory of the would-be liberator of slaves – and writing his army serial number for the passport number. The symbolism is reinforced by his stopping work on the symphony, "Queen of Sheba", and going back to the theme he had called "Arbeit und Rhythmus" but which he now calls "The Body and Soul of John Brown". Again, visiting with Genevieve Rod, he has the wild desire to jump up and shout,

"Look at me; I'm a deserter. I'm under the wheels of your system. If your system doesn't succeed in killing me, it will be that much weaker, it will have less strength to kill others." [41]

This passage serves both as exposition of Andrews' feelings toward the society from which he is now cut off and as a reference to the structural pattern of the novel. If anything, the intent is too obvious.

Genevieve Rod, who is sympathetic toward Andrews as an artist and who represents the attitude of society toward him, cannot understand his desertion. The last time she sees him, she indicates that she has already dismissed him from the world of the living. She says, ". . . Oh, this is so frightful. You would have

[41] *Ibid.*, p. 455.

been a great composer. I feel sure of it." [42] After this, the only thing left is for the M.P.'s to come to get him, leaving "The Body and Soul of John Brown" to be scattered by the wind. Andrews is back "under the wheels".

The motif suggested by the music Andrews is writing about the Queen of Sheba as she is pictured in Flaubert's *La Tentation de Saint Antoine* is symbolic of several passions that counterpoint the restrictions imposed by the "machine". Thus, the Queen of Sheba represents not merely the freedom of the artist, but also an unrestricted, Byronic romanticism that includes everything from personal liberty to pure sex:

The Queen of Sheba, grotesque as a satyr, white flaming with worlds of desire, as the great implacable Aphrodite, stood with her hand on his shoulder sending shivers of warm sweetness rippling through his body, while her voice intoned in his ears all the inexhaustable voluptuousness of life.[43]

Contrasting with the recurring image of the Queen of Sheba is a phrase which to Andrews represents all that is cruel and brutal in the army. The first time he is apprehended by M.P.'s, an officer says, "One of you men teach him to salute", and an M.P. beats him unmercifully.[44] These two images evoke emotions and responses from Andrews that are the expression of the two conflicting forces in his life.

Another recurring theme in *Three Soldiers* is developed through the "Y" men who, contrary to what they affirm, are invariably hate mongers of the first order. Dos Passos uses them as an example of the contrast between ideal and application in which an institution works against the very principles on which it is founded. In the debates between Andrews and the "Y" men, he invariably makes them reveal their bigotry and stupidity. They are, in fact, so generally despicable that one suspects the author's objectivity.

The first appearance of the theme is a "Y" man telling a group of singing soldiers to put "lots more guts in the get and lots of kill

[42] *Ibid.*, p. 465.
[43] *Ibid.*, p. 240. *See* also pp. 211, 213, 217-218, 256-257, and 313.
[44] *Ibid.*, p. 387. *See* also pp. 403, 410, 412, and 470.

in the Kaiser".[45] Beginning with this repelling introduction, the
theme culminates in the visit of a "Y" man, obviously a minis-
ter, to Andrews in the hospital. The "Y" man begins a discussion
of which the burden is hate for Germans. When Andrews
interrupts him to suggest that if he hates the Germans so much,
he should borrow a revolver from an officer and kill some prisoners
of war who work around the hospital, the man indignantly replies
that Andrews can't be much of a Christian. Andrews sarcastically
answers, "*I* make no pretensions to Christianity." [46]

The only other significant theme in the novel is one of revolution, of which Dos Passos has said,

Any spring is a time of overturn, but then Lenin was alive, the Seattle
general strike had seemed the beginning of the flood instead of the
beginning of the ebb. . . . in every direction the countries of the world
stretched out starving and angry, ready for anything turbulent and
new. . . . It wasn't that today was any finer than it is now, it's perhaps
that tomorrow seemed vaster. . . .[47]

It has also been pointed out that Dos Passos was already becoming attracted to revolutionary doctrine when he wrote *Three
Soldiers* and that he was writing it while traveling in the Spain of
Pio Baroja, of whom he had written a glowing account as a "Novelist of the Revolution" in *Rosinante to the Road Again*.[48] It is
doubtful, however, that temporary environment could make so
much difference; at best the evidence is purely circumstantial.

In the first part of the book, the revolutionary theme is carried
by Eisenstein, a man in Fuselli's company who has long, dreary
conversations with a French revolutionist. Fuselli is sometimes
drawn into their conversations to show, by his ardent conformity
to the system as it is, the hopelessness of their dreams. The theme
is picked up again after Andrews has deserted. He then becomes
the spokesman for the revolution, but even at the last, revolution
is presented merely as an indefinite hope. In the last reference to
this theme, Chrisfield asks Andrews if

[45] *Ibid.*, p. 22.
[46] *Ibid.*, p. 224.
[47] "Introduction", *Three Soldiers*, p. v.
[48] Walter B. Rideout, *The Radical Novel in the United States 1900-1954*
(Cambridge, Harvard University Press, 1956), p. 157.

"... there's anything in that revolution business? Ah hadn't never thought they could buck the system thataway."

"They did in Russia."

"Then we'd be free, civilians, like we all was before the draft. But that ain't possible Andy! That ain't possible Andy!"

"We'll see," said Andrews. . . .[49]

The improvement of Dos Passos' skills as a novelist in *Three Soldiers* has already been largely demonstrated in his greater attention to structure and continuity of narrative, his realistic conversations, his use of symbols, his more definite presentation of themes, and his use of irony and contrast. Another area where Dos Passos reveals marked improvement is in the skill of rendering emotions, although he does a better job with Chrisfield than with the more articulate Andrews. Once, for example, when the regiment has been marching all day, Chrisfield has a sprained ankle, and his woolen tunic is too hot and too tight.

Chrisfield marched with his fists clenched; he wanted to fight somebody, to run his bayonet into a man as he ran it into the dummy in that everlasting bayonet drill, he wanted to strip himself naked, to squeeze the wrists of a girl until she screamed.

They pass another company, and Chrisfield sees his enemy, Sergeant Anderson, "... but Sergeant Anderson did not seem to recognize him. It gave him a dull angry feeling as if he'd been cut by a friend." The explosion occurs when the troops finally halt:

"What are you dreamin' about, Indiana?" said Judkins punching Chrisfield jovially in the ribs.

Chrisfield doubled his fists and gave him a smashing blow in the jaw that Judkins warded off just in time.[50]

Another device which is more frequently used in some of the later novels is the telescoped dream in which Dos Passos gathers the basic conflicts within the individual, his emotional responses, and the trivial incidents of daily life into a nightmare. Dos Passos' use of imagery also shows improvement in this novel. The images, usually involving or ending with a simile, show an in-

---

[49] *Three Soldiers*, p. 440.
[50] *Ibid.*, pp. 160-161.

creasing attention to mass and color. In the following image, he blocks out the large masses of form and color and then adds the details:

At the head of an alley he came out on a terrace. Beyond the strong curves of the pattern of the iron balustrade was an expanse of country, pale green, falling to blue towards the horizon, patched with pink and slatecolored houses and carved with railway tracks. At his feet the Seine shone like a curved sword blade.[51]

Another type of image which Dos Passos develops in this novel is the sudden "still" image which momentarily freezes men in motion. In the following example, he captures the image as well as the response of the character involved in it:

The column shifted over to the side of the road to avoid a train of motor trucks going the other way. Chrisfield felt the heavy mud spurt up over him as truck after truck rumbled by. With the wet back of one hand he tried to wipe it off his face, but the grit, when he rubbed it, hurt his skin, made tender by the rain. He swore long and whiningly, half aloud. His rifle felt as heavy as an iron girder.[52]

When he finished *Three Soldiers*, Dos Passos had already found some of his major themes, he had begun his experiments with structure, and he was thoroughly familiar with most of the narrative skills that he would continue to employ with increasing dexterity. There remained only one false start in *Streets of Night* as he shifted from the backdrop of the army and war to that of metropolitan city life before he would write his first significant novel, *Manhattan Transfer*.

3

Between the publication of *Three Soldiers* in 1921 and the publication of *Streets of Night* in 1923, Dos Passos published *A Pushcart at the Curb* and *Rosinante to the Road Again*. *A Pushcart at the Curb*[53] is Dos Passos' only volume of poetry, but it was a

[51] *Ibid.*, p. 373.

[52] *Ibid.*, p. 141.

[53] John Dos Passos, *A Pushcart at the Curb* (New York, George H. Doran Company, 1922).

significant publication because poetry was never far from the surface during the years of the most notable productions. Beginning with *Manhattan Transfer* and ending with *The Grand Design,* Dos Passos wrote seven consecutive novels in which he used poetry or, as some term it, "prose poems", and although he dropped the practice for a time, he resumed it again when he wrote *Mid-century* (1961). The major importance of the poetry to *Streets of Night,* and to all the subsequent novels for that matter, is the sharpening of images and the economy of words for the setting of scenes.

Rosinante to the Road Again, a hybrid of such varied antecedents as the travel book, social and cultural history, literary criticism, and narrative fiction, is a fascinating study of structural experimentation and will be discussed from that standpoint later. But for even a cursory discussion of theme and subject matter of any novel from *Streets of Night* forward, certain comments made by Dos Passos in *Rosinante to the Road Again* must be considered. Having exhausted his war experiences in his first two novels, Dos Passos turned back to the main stream of American life for his subject matter. In so doing, he was giving himself further opportunity to deal directly with problems of economics, politics, social ethics, and such like – all topics which he had touched on in his war novels. He was sympathetic with the idealistic anarchists – but not the bomb-throwing ones – and although he was never the ardent supporter of communism that many believed him to be, he was for some ten or twelve years after World War I at least willing to see what reforms in society and government they might effect. His familiarity, then, with the approach to history and to social evolution employed by these groups – the habit of viewing the whole fabric of a civilization as part of a great, continuous process – led him to take the same approach to his art. This concept of art as the "natural history" of society was not casually achieved, but was conceived with care and deliberation. He calls to mind the writing of Balzac, and in a selection of literary criticism dealing with Pio Baroja, for example, he concludes,

In the end it is rather natural history than dramatic creation. But a natural history that gives you the pictures etched with vitriol of

Spanish life in the end of the nineteenth and the beginning of the twentieth century which you get in these novels of Baroja's is very near the highest sort of creation.[54]

And in one other passage – this one from his discussion of Blasco Ibanez but pertaining directly to the needs of American literature – he says,

We need writing that shall be acid, with sharp edges on it, yeasty to leaven the lump of glucose that the combination of the ideals of the man in the swivelchair with decayed puritanism has made of our national consciousness.[55]

Thus he suggests that a "natural history" which gives a picture of a national life is "very near the highest sort of creation", and that the particular dosage needed by America is one which will be both sharp and leavening in nature. America needed then, according to Dos Passos, novels like *Manhattan Transfer* and *U.S.A.*

Streets of Night does not satisfy the requirements laid down by the author. It is too narrow in its social implication, too introspective to be the "natural history" of a culture. The most striking thing about the novel is the close resemblance it bears in theme and in characterization to the early works of T. S. Eliot, which Dos Passos had already read.[56] The three central characters are of the intellectual class of a dying culture; they are Eliot's "hollow men" living in a "wasteland" and victimized by their own conformity. They, too, come and go, "talking of Michaelangelo". Each, like Prufrock, has an opportunity to choose between a sterile existence and a vital one; and each, like Prufrock, lets the moment slip without taking action.

Once again Dos Passos had written a book which was composed of a series of incidents rather than a continuing narrative, but what most weakens the book is that the theme is carried more through the failure of the characters to achieve relationships with each other or with the world – they cannot even communicate clearly with one another – than through character development,

---

[54] John Dos Passos, *Rosinante to the Road Again* (New York, George H. Doran Company, 1922), p. 99.
[55] *Ibid.*, p. 131.
[56] Letter dated March 5, 1961, John Dos Passos to John D. Brantley.

plot, or structure. The result is almost an inadvertant parody of the quasi-serious romance – as if Faith Baldwin had attempted to write in the style of Checkhov. Another weakness lies in the form chosen to carry the theme. Prufrock hesitates on the verge of life for only 131 lines; Dos Passos' characters hesitate for more than 300 pages. One grows weary.

The three principal characters of *Streets of Night* are Fanshaw Macdougan, David Wendell, and Nancibel Taylor who are close friends living in Boston in the first decade of the twentieth century. Fanshaw is first introduced as a college student and later as an art instructor. Fanshaw's given name may be a deliberate attempt to bring to mind the idealistic central character in Nathaniel Hawthorne's first novel. "Wenny" is a slightly younger man who from time to time mentions that he is working on a Master of Arts degree in anthropology. "Nan" talks a great deal about working on her "career" as a violinist. The three friends have innumerable walks, teas, and dinners together, often reminiscent of a play by Checkhov where the characters sit around trying to explain themselves but where no one listens to what the others are saying. Their basic condition is isolation, but they are not suffering existential *weltschmertz*; their reactions are emotional and Freudian rather than philosophical and are so completely defined by the author as to leave no room for speculation.

Wendell is the character nearest to Prufrock in the early chapters because he is awake as Prufrock is awake to the artificiality of their lives, and he wishes to be out of it. Wenny frequently drinks, he wants to "pick up" a girl but never accomplishes that but once, and, finally, he drops out of school, hoping thus to become part of life. He proposes to Nan, whom he loves passionately, but she is unable to respond; he has a seaman's card, but his job is tutoring a young man in school; he makes his "pick up" but he cannot go through with the affair; he commits suicide successfully.

Nan, who talks a great deal about her career but gets nowhere with it, is, if anything, more attracted to Wendell than he to her. The excuse she gives herself for rejecting him is that she must let nothing interfere with her career. She thus ends as a violinist who will never be more than second violin in a lady's group; the woman that she might have been can turn only to the cold comfort of a Ouija board in hope of contacting Wendell's sterile ghost. The symbolism is not especially subtle.

Fanshaw, hounded by the ugliness of this world and by the beauties of the world of the Renaissance, finds his life complicated by an extremely possessive mother, by an almost homosexual attachment for Wendell, by a "pure" and "beautiful" love for Nan, by normal sex drives, and by his fear of having to come to grips with life. After Wendell's death, Fanshaw proposes to Nan, but they do not marry. He goes overseas during World War I, but even the experiences of the war followed by a night in a house of prostitution are not enough to shake him out of the pattern in which his life has been cast.

The theme of cultural disentigration is clearly expressed through frequent contrasts between the empty ennui of the Twentieth Century and the full vitality of the Renaissance, but the novel fails in its amateurish dialogue, in its overdrawn imagery, in its heavy handed symbolism, and in its very flow of words. In style and technique, the book is much closer to the worst excesses in *One Man's Initiation-1917* than to anything before or after it. In this novel the "machine" is the society of the Boston-Harvard environment, and the theme is developed through the efforts of the three principal characters to break the constricting molds into which that society casts them. They fail because they cannot bear to face reality and because they seek refuge in something as false as that from which they flee.

Each of the characters in turn merges his consciousness with the realities of life at least temporarily. Wenny has already come to an understanding of the condition of their lives when the novel begins, and he makes the first real effort to break the pattern of negation and rejection. Much of his character is implicit in his explanation of a violent argument with his father:

My father and I had a little chat about life and eternity. . . . I laid on for life and he laid on for eternity. . . . Naturally, being a clergyman, eternity is his line of goods. We got sore. I'm never going to take anything more from him, either money or his insolence."

"But how are you going to live?" cried Fanshaw.

"What the hell? I've got as much muscle as the next man." [57]

Wenny *would* act, but he is not quite the man of action he feels himself to be in a moment of irritation. In some respects he is a good deal like Tom in Dos Passos' play *The Garbage Man,* which was written the same year that *Streets of Night* was published. Tom, who told himself that "the moon was a silver gong" and who wanted to "climb high enough to beat on it with both hands" to make all of his wishes come true,[58] later admits that he has ". . . always just looked on. I've never done anything but make up lies." [59] Wenny's failure is of the same type. Once he tells Nan:

"Before I came to college I spent my time dreaming, and now I spend it gabbling about my dreams that have died and begun to stink. Why the only genuine thing I ever did in my life was get drunk, and I haven't done that often." [60]

So despite his dreams, Wenny cannot extricate himself from the web of his society. He cannot get a job outside of the college; he cannot gain the courage to leave Boston; Nan rejects his proposal of marriage; he cannot stay with the prostitute; and he bitterly hates his father, whom he blames for his weakness. Just before he commits suicide, he sums up his failure as well as his desire for oblivion:

I have nerve enough for this, why not for the rest; for shipping on a windjammer, for walking with Nan down streets unaccountable and dark between blind brick walls that tremble with the roar of engines, for her seagrey eyes in my eyes, her lips, the sweetish fatty smell of Ellen's lips. Maybe death's all that, sinking into the body of a dark woman, with proud cold thighs, hair black, black.[61]

There is never any doubt about Nan's feeling for Wenny. She undergoes a violent emotional upheaval almost every time she sees him:

[57] John Dos Passos, *Streets of Night* (New York, George H. Doran Company, 1934), pp. 100-101.
[58] John Dos Passos, *Three Plays* (New York, Harcourt, Brace and Company, 1934), p. 1.
[59] *Ibid.,* "The Garbage Man", part 3, scene 2, p. 54.
[60] *Streets of Night,* p. 192.
[61] *Ibid.,* pp. 200-201.

"Gosh! The size of that star," came Wenny's voice from the window. In his black silhouette Nan was imagining the moulding of the muscles of the arms, the hollow between the shoulders, the hard bulge of calves. . . . The little demon in her head was hissing Careful Nancibel, careful Nancibel, as she walked over to the window. Her arm hanging limply at her side touched his arm; writhing hump-backed flares danced an insane ballet through her body.[62]

Wendell represents life to Nan; he is the one means by which she might give some meaning to her existence, but she rejects him, using her "career" as a rationalization, because she is afraid of life. In her rejection of life Nan is compared with her Aunt "M" whose story of her "young man" is basically that of the failure of Nan and Wendell. After she hears her aunt's story, Nan almost, but not quite, has the courage to face the truth: "And I will be like that, spending my life explaining why I didn't live." Thus she sees the reality of her life. But the sight is more than she can accept so she immediately returns to her self deception; "No! No! Poor Aunt M. had nothing to fall back on. I have my music, my career, my sense of humor. . . ." [63] Yet within minutes of her self-assurance, she thinks she sees Wendell on the street and "Dizzy blackness welled up through her". She calls aloud to him before she can check herself, and finally runs home, "spun in the grip of a horrible nausea". Nan's failure to live is also developed through contrast with Mabel Worthington who, also a violinist in a woman's orchestra, had run away with an Italian laborer who "looked like a Greek God" but who was already married. When Nancibel meets her, she has borne a child; she has married a "Dutchman" for his money; and she has already established herself as an agent for other musicians and is considering a singing career for herself. Nan's reaction to this very vital woman is to hurry home to her Ouija board.

Fanshaw, like Nan, is incapable of taking action or of meeting the demands of a vital existence. Even as an undergraduate, he is already afraid to act, already dreaming. In a long passage compounded of reality, memories, and daydreams, Dos Passos, skillfully exposing Fanshaw's consciousness, paints a vivid picture of

[62] *Ibid.*, p. 37.
[63] *Ibid.*, p. 259.

the sophomore mind.[64] The author's purpose is to show Fanshaw as a young man already failing to act in life, already beginning to rationalize his failure, already burying his emotions under a layer of stuffiness. The possessiveness of Fanshaw's mother is another deterrent to life for him. She tells him, "I was thinking, Fanshaw, supposing you married and some dreadful woman won you away from your poor mother; what should I do? You're so sweet to me; you take such care of me", and she adds, "They are such scheming creatures, so deceitful and wicked, and I so want you to have a beautiful career and be a comfort to me." [65] Fanshaw takes refuge in the sterile remnants of the past, constantly comparing the luxuriance and the richness of renaissance life as depicted in the art of that period with the life he sees about him. The comparisons are made in a spirit similar to that in T. S. Eliot's *Wasteland*:

"Cultivated people in this generation," he was saying, "Are like foreigners who suddenly find themselves in a country whose language they do not know, whose institutions they do not understand, like people in one of those great state barges the Venetians had, that Canaletto drew so well. . . ."[66]

Fanshaw's attitude toward sex and marriage is given specific expression in four separate scenes, each portrayed in terms of contrast. He is first contrasted with Cham Mason, his undergraduate roommate, when they take two show girls to Norumbega Park. There Cham quickly seduces his girl, but Fanshaw is afraid and leaves his girl crying because she isn't having a good time. Later, when Cham marries, Fanshaw first has to listen to the smutty stories and suggestions of others in the wedding party, and then, after the wedding, he takes a walk in the garden, only to be confronted by a couple in a passionate embrace. Fanshaw flees from the scene which gives him a momentary glimpse of himself:

And the years slip by like telegraph poles past you in the train and people marry and spoon on benches and I'm always alone, moral, refined, restrained. If I were only made like Wenny, I'd enjoy life.

[64] *Ibid.*, pp. 28-30.
[65] *Ibid.*, pp. 95-97.
[66] *Ibid.*, p. 155.

but he quickly adds,

> Disgusting, though, out in the open like that where anybody could see,
> worse than factory hands at Norumbega.
>   One must try to be beautiful about life.[67]

His attitude toward sex and marriage is also contrasted with that
of Wendell. The first pointed comparison occurs when Wendell
persuades Nan and Fanshaw to go with him to a "girlie" show.
Wendell is fascinated, but Fanshaw feels only revulsion, and he
leaves. Nan makes no comment about the show, but she follows Fanshaw out, indicating her rejection as well. Another obvious point of comparison between Wendell and Fanshaw is the
proposal that each makes to Nan. The intensity of Wendell's emotions renders him almost incoherent at times, and although she
refuses him, Nan's emotional response is equally violent. But
Fanshaw, during the taking of tea, very deliberately, though
hesitantly – because he, like Prufrock, fears rejection as much as
he fears acceptance – weaves his proposal into a two page conversation which reaches its peak of emotion for both Nan and
himself when he covers her hand with his and says, "Dear Nan".
They call off their marriage without ever talking about it directly
just as they had agreed to marry without ever talking about it
directly; besides that, Nan never registers anything but a "sane"
feeling in the presence of Fanshaw.

Fanshaw's last opportunity to choose between life and mere
existence occurs when he is ready to return to the United States
after serving with the Red Cross in Europe. After he is already
on the boat, he is tempted to get off, to do "one crazy thing in a
lifetime", but he hasn't the courage to carry out the temptation.
As the boat stands out to the channel, he is thinking,

> And I'll go back and go to and fro to lectures with a notebook under
> my arm, and now and then in the evening, when I haven't any engage-
> ment, walk into Boston through terrible throbbing streets and think
> for a moment I have Nan and Wenny with me, and that we are young,
> leansouled people out of the Renaissance, ready to divide life like a
> cake with our strong hands.[68]

[67] *Ibid.*, p. 159-160.
[68] *Ibid.*, pp. 310-311.

But the reader does not think the mermaids will sing to Fanshaw, either.

Besides the extensive use of the interior monologue, such as the agonizing self-appraisals of Fanshaw, Dos Passos also makes considerable use of contrast in *Streets of Night*. The central theme is expressed in terms of contrast: between action and failure to act, between life and mere existence. Virtually every scene, every episode, every character invites comparison and contrast with another. The symbolism in this novel is actually more restrained than in the preceeding novels, but because the imagery in which the symbols are set is so lush, the symbol itself appears as obvious as any encountered in the two preceeding novels. For example:

Somewhere at the end of a long corridor of her mind she ran through the dappled shadow of woods, naked, swift, chased by someone brown, flushed, goatfooted. She could feel in her nostrils the roughness of the smell of Wenny's damp homespun suit.[69]

Sex is the controlling symbol throughout the novel. It is symbolic of life, and every emotional response related to sex is indicative of a desire for life; every overt act related to sex symbolizes participation in life; and every submersion of emotion and every rejection of opportunity to act symbolizes rejection of life. So it is that each of the three characters has a moment of reality in which he recognizes his life for what it actually is, but each fails to break the pattern into which he has been cast by the social machine. Thus, instead of the *lived* life, they substitute a Ouija board, suicide, and some lectures on renaissance art.

4

Manhattan Transfer (1925) has no narrative in the ordinary sense of the word, and the theme, while it is well established, has no great movement of its own; rather, like the so-called thesis novel, the theme is conceived in its entirety from the first page: it is the emptiness of society and culture as revealed through individual

[69] *Ibid.*, p. 44.

lives in the wasteland of the twentieth century. Unlike most thesis novels, however, the "proof" is not developed in a narrative but is established through a series of some two hundred episodes, many of which have no direct relation to other episodes except as they all are related to the theme. These episodes are carefully spaced for continuity of narrative and contrast and suggest four major flaws in people who are the products of Twentieth Century urban society: (1) a primary interest in self and a lack of concern for others, (2) materialism, (3) shallowness and hypocrisy, and (4) cynicism.

In this novel, Dos Passos is more interested in recording society than in explaining it, more interested in its being than in its becoming. He is attempting a chapter of the natural history of a society that he had mentioned in his discussion of Baroja in *Rosinante to the Road Again.* The "revolutionary" theme that critics titilate themselves with in this novel is much more a whisper than a shout. There are, in fact, five rather stereotyped anarchist and communist statements. There are no communists worth noting, and the anarchist who speaks loudest in the first part of the book is a wealthy capitalist at the end.

The isolation of the individual in the machine-like metropolitan life is treated with more emphasis than any political idea and is revealed as the source of the complementary social ailments – self-interest and loss of social conscience. Ed Thatcher's behavior as he passes the vicinity of a tenement fire is typical of this theme as it is portrayed in *Manhattan Transfer:*

Thatcher was working his way out of the crowd. At the corner a man was looking into the fire alarm box. As Thatcher brushed past him he caught a smell of coaloil from the man's clothes. The man looked up into his face with a smile. He had tallowy sagging cheeks and bright popeyes. Thatcher's hands and feet went suddenly cold. The firebug. The papers say they hang around like that to watch it. He walked home fast, ran up the stairs, and locked the door behind him.[70]

Although he has been a witness to the death and destruction

[70] John Dos Passos, *Manhattan Transfer* (Boston, Houghton Mifflin Company, 1925), p. 14.

caused by the fire, Thatcher's concern is not the social one of apprehending the firebug, but the selfish one of seeking security in his own burrow.

George Baldwin, a lawyer, is another example of this type of behavior. He seduces the wife of his first client, but when, at the termination of the case, his chances for professional success have greatly improved, he breaks off with her. When she leaves him for the last time, his only reaction is to say, "Oh well, that's that", and he goes back to working on the preparation of a brief.[71] Thinking back over the affair some years later, he can't even remember her name, although it was his first case and he has had more or less continual business with the woman's husband from that time forward. Once she has served her purpose in his life, he simply forgets her.

The instances are many. When Bud Lorpenning commits suicide by jumping off a bridge, he lands in the water near a tugboat. The Captain of the boat exhibits no sympathy. His whole reaction is one of selfinterest; he groans, "God damn it to hell. ... A pretty thing to happen on a man's wedding day." [72] And when destitute Joe Harland, the former Wall Street tycoon, calls on a former employee to borrow twenty-five dollars, he is refused although the man had liked Joe well enough previously to name a son after him. The refusal forces Joe to beg, and the man moves "back against the wall as if to ward off a blow", and then gives Joe fifty cents.[73] Perhaps the most ironic of all such instances is that concerning Tony Hunter and Nevada Jones. Nevada, George Baldwin's mistress, has been trying to cure Tony Hunter of his homosexual tendencies and has been using Baldwin to help Tony in his theatrical career. When Baldwin catches the two of them together, he breaks off his relations with Nevada, who accepts the situation philosophically, but Tony turns bitterly on Nevada, "But you're not thinking of my career. ... Women are so selfish. If you hadn't led me on. ..." [74]

---

[71] *Ibid.*, p. 92.
[72] *Ibid.*, p. 126.
[73] *Ibid.*, p. 160.
[74] *Ibid.*, p. 335.

The materialism of the age, another major area of Dos Passos' theme, is revealed through the obsession of the characters with "getting ahead". There is real estate speculation as well as speculation on Wall Street, the latter being reduced to absurdity by Joe Harland's insistence that neither skill nor brains, but an old tie was responsible for his success. The whole career of James Merivale, who begins as a child by playing a game called "stock market" and whose successful career at least partially depends upon his allowing his sister to marry a bigamist, reaches its apex when he sits in the "Metropolitan Club" smoking a thirty-five cent cigar reading the *Wall Street Journal*. There are also a number of peripheral episodes related to the same theme, such as those of Jake Silverman and the firm of Blackhead and Densch in which business failure is directly the result of speculation or improper use of funds. The shallowness and hypocrisy of the age is attested time and again. When the show girl Fifi Waters demonstrates her high kick, the man whose hat she kicks off cries out, "For crissake, you kicked me in the eye". The implied insult to the accuracy and heighth of her kick causes her to burst into tears and exclaim, "I won't be insulted like that".[75] She is not concerned that the man may lose his eye.

Jimmy Herf, who often serves as a commentator, cries out to his friend, Stan,

"Well perhaps you can tell me why in this country nobody ever does anything. Nobody ever writes any music or starts any revolutions or falls in love. All anybody ever does is to get drunk and tell smutty stories. I think it's disgusting. . . ." [76]

It is only a little while after this that Dos Passos introduces the broadly humorous spectacle of Ellen and Stan's lovemaking being interrupted by her husband, "Jojo", who is a homosexual. The episode explores the shallows of Twentieth Century morality to their slightest depths.

The hypocrisy of the age is exploited in such episodes as that in which a woman gives Hotel Aster as her address rather than her true residence in the Bronx, in James Merivale's prostitution

[75] *Ibid.*, p. 34.
[76] *Ibid.*, p. 193.

of his own sister because her bigamist-bridegroom can introduce him to important businessmen, and in the beautifully rendered dialogue between Gus McNiel and a political underling:

"Say Joey how'll you boys line up on the mayoralty election?"
"That depends on the general attitude towards the needs of the ex-service man. . . ."
"Look here Joey you're a smart feller. . . ."
"Oh they'll line up all right. I kin talk em around." [77]

Thus are the votes delivered. An ironic touch is added moments later when Joey meets one of his subordinates.

"Gus tells me Tammany'll be right behind us in our drive for the bonus . . . planning a nation wide campaign." . . . Opposite the old City Hall there was a scaffolding. Joe pointed at it with his cigar. "That there's the new statue of Civic Virtue the mayor's havin' set up." [78]

The theme of cynicism is further exploited in such flippant remarks as Baldwin's about a man named Specker who is the "only honest man in the city of New York". Says Baldwin, "He's never made anything much by it." [79] Ellen says "Jojo" is her husband, "till divorce do us part," [80] and Jimmy Herf and Ellen are told that "the difficulty under prohibition is keeping sober".[81] Perhaps the thing that makes the cynicism of the characters such an acid social commentary is that their cynical attitudes are usually well founded. Phineas Blackhead, after a political argument with his partner Densch, tells his daughter,

"If you ever hear a man talking about his duty as a citizen, by the living Jingo don't trust him. . . . He's up to some kind of monkey business nine times out of ten." [82]

It is shortly after this event that Densch justifies Blackhead's estimation by deserting the firm when it is having financial difficulties, thereby insuring its failure.

[77] *Ibid.*, p. 315.
[78] *Ibid.*, p. 316.
[79] *Ibid.*, p. 75.
[80] *Ibid.*, p. 139.
[81] *Ibid.*, p. 279.
[82] *Ibid.*, p. 328.

The attitudes of the characters towards their environment reveal something about both the characters and the environment. Gus McNeil, a newly married milk man, dreams of taking his wife, Nellie, out to the free land in North Dakota where he can raise wheat, and he says, "This here livin' in the city's no good." [83] But Gus McNiel, the well-established political boss, never talks about leaving the city. The mature George Baldwin, too, will not consider leaving New York. He tells Ellen,

"The terrible thing about having New York go stale on you is that there's nowhere else. It's the top of the world. All we can do is go round and round in a squirrel cage." [84]

Jimmy Herf, who often serves as the chorus, is the most prolific commentator on the city and the culture it represents. Not long before he leaves the city, he explains, "I'm beginning to learn a few of the things I don't want. . . . At least I'm beginning to have the nerve to admit to myself how much I dislike all the things I don't want." [85] Perhaps the sharpest criticism of the city implied in Herf's thinking is his eventual realization that for him there are but two alternatives: "go away in a dirty soft shirt or stay in a clean arrow collar".[86] Jimmy hitches a ride out of town and tells the driver he is going "pretty far".[87] Thus he has comprehended the reality that is himself and his environment and, unlike the spiritual anemics in *Streets of Night*, he takes a positive step by breaking free from the constricting "machine".

Manhattan Transfer has been called "collectivist" and even described as "revolutionary". More accurately, it has been pointed out that "Even the radicals, the Anarchists or Communists who appear occasionally in these pages, are trapped".[88] Actually, in the vision of Twentieth Century life portrayed in *Manhattan Transfer*, the radicals and Anarchists and Communists had to take their chances along with the ordinary capitalists. The first serious portrayal of the Anarchist theme occurs in the episode

[83] *Ibid.*, p. 46.
[84] *Ibid.*, p. 220.
[85] *Ibid.*, p. 360.
[86] *Ibid.*, pp. 365-366.
[87] *Ibid.*, p. 404.
[88] Rideout, p. 150.

where Marco, the old waiter, consoles Congo for having been cheated out of his wages:

"It's the same all over the world, the police beating us up, rich people cheating us out of their starvation wages, and who's fault? ... Dio cane! Your fault, my fault, Emile's fault. ...."
    "We didn't make the world. ... They did or maybe God did."
    "God's on their side, like a policeman. ... When the day comes we'll kill God ... I am an anarchist."

Congo bitterly replies,

"... I haven't any money and I haven't any work. Look at that." Congo pointed with a dirty finger to a long rip on his trouserknee. "That's anarchist. ... Hell, I'm going out to Senegal and get to be a nigger." [89]

Congo is also used to portray the anarchist attitude toward war. This is shown in his declaration that he won't go because "A workingman has no country". He goes on to give the stereotyped explanation of war:

"You know why they have this here war. ... So that workingman all over won't make big revolution ... Too busy fighting. So Guillaume and Viviani and l'Empereur dAutriche and Krupp and Rothschild and Morgan they say let's have a war. ...." [90]

But Congo fights in the war and loses a leg in Italy during his tour of duty, and – through his machinations during the days of prohibition – he finally rises to wealth in a shockingly capitalistic way. And so go the Anarchists.

    The first really strong communist view is given in a scene consisting of a streetcorner orator, complete with soapbox, who makes the usual spiel to the "wageslaves" about the various forms of capitalistic tyranny and concludes with an obvious comparison between the Russian peasant and the American worker which implies the necessity of revolution without stating it. Then the man picks up his box and walks off. A few people listen to him, but there is no indication that he has influenced anyone. Since the device is used as a chapter head, it is not incorporated directly into the lives of any of the characters; it merely forms a back-

---

[89] *Manhatten Transfer*, p. 37.
[90] *Ibid.*, p. 117.

drop. There is also Elmer, the communist labor organizer, who wants the workers to see that they are in a "class war" and who talks of a strike as the "worker's university". But his stereotyped urgings convince neither his girl friend nor the reader; he is too much of a caricature. The portrait of the intellectual communist is of the same variety. Jimmy Herf hears the man's talk and agrees with him that there is need for some readjustment of government and society, but when the discussion ends, Herf's reaction indicates that he has not accepted much doctrine:

> "Oh gosh, things are rotten," he said. "God, I wish I could blame it all on capitalism the way Martin does." [91]

Two examples of injustice mentioned in the book, the unprovoked arrest of the three innocent Italians and the deportation of the communists, are sometimes cited as examples of Dos Passos' anarchist or communist feelings. But the real events which served as the base for these episodes in the novel were such gross violations of the constitutional rights of American citizens, that many of the very tamest liberals were moved to outrage.

The unity of impression which is achieved in *Manhattan Transfer* would have been impossible had the book been given a structural arrangement based on anything but theme. It is always theme which determines which character and what episode is to be presented. This method is an adaptation of a device that Dos Passos uses in most of his books. In *Three Soldiers* he had shifted his angle of narration, in *Rosinante to the Road Again* he had alternated essay with narrative, and in *Manhattan Transfer* he juxtaposes many concurrent narrative fragments, each with its own continuing angle of narration. It is noteworthy that if all of the narratives related from the viewpoint of any one character were put together in sequence, the result would still not constitute an adequately developed plot. Each part is nothing without the whole; each part is necessary to the complete picture of the whole. The chance mingling of the lives of the characters, an increasingly common device in the works of Dos Passos from *Three Soldiers* forward, is not outside the realm of possibility

---

[91] *Ibid.*, p. 165.

and is necessary if he is to approach his theme from multiple viewpoints and yet maintain coherence. Dos Passos' attention to unity is emphasized in that in 1924 he published a short story called "July" [92] which concerns Jimmy Herf and his Merivale relatives. For two important reasons Dos Passos, a man never hesitant about publishing anything in three or four different places, did not include the story in *Manhattan Transfer*. In the first place, the setting of the story is in Virginia, which would have violated the unity of place, and would have been the only such violation; in the second place, the story, while it adds emphasis to the contrast between the characters of Jimmy Herf and James Merivale, really adds nothing essentially new to the character of either.

Among the more important devices are the lyric and lyric-prose passages at the beginning of each chapter. These passages – composed of poetry, extended images, vignettes, advertisements, headlines, titles and lines of popular songs, and catch phrases – serve a number of purposes. They are invariably tied to the text of the novel itself, either in the chapter to which they are appended or to another chapter, usually the preceeding or succeeding one. They sometimes serve as an expansion of the idea suggested by a chapter title; and they, together with dozens of incidental references in the text, serve to link the narrative to specific moments in time. The similarity of these passages to the "Camera Eye" and "Newsreel" sections of *U.S.A.* is obvious.

Characterization in a novel such as *Manhattan Transfer* is a special problem. Since there is little space for extensive analysis, motivation must be compressed. Ellen's insecurity is implicit in her desire not to grow up and in her sleeping with her knees drawn up to her chin in the pre-natal position whenever she is afraid or undergoing emotional stress. The Joyce touch noted by some critics is perhaps most evident in the stream of consciousness passages such as Stan's as he commits suicide, and James Merivale's final musings on his successful career. The use of Jimmy Herf as the idealistic individual who acts both as a central character and as a spokesman for the author is indicative that Dos

[92] John Dos Passos, "July", *The Transatlantic Review*, II (August, 1924), pp. 154-179.

Passos had not entirely freed himself in *Manhattan Transfer* from association with character and theme. A comparison of Herf with Martin Howe and John Andrews, however, is sufficient to reveal a strong movement toward objectivity in which the idealist is still present but in which the character's behavior constitutes his comment on society, and perception is left to the reader.

Blanche Gelfant's study of the symbolism in *Manhattan Transfer* makes further discussion of the subject niggling.[93] If she misses anything at all, it is perhaps the similarity between some of Dos Passos' symbols and some of Eliot's in *The Wasteland*.

When Dos Passos completed *Manhattan Transfer,* he was showing more and more interest in the relation of the individual to the "machine" and had developed three basic patterns of reaction to it. First, there is the pattern set by James Merivale who never merges his consciousness with reality and who thus never recognizes the manner in which he prostitutes himself to the dictates of the "machine". Second, there is the pattern of Jimmy Herf who apprehends reality and who takes steps to escape from the "machine". And, third, there is the pattern of John Andrews who perceives the reality of the "machine", who rejects existence in a world containing it, and who thus seeks escape by oblivion as a martyred idealist. Dos Passos had also learned to experiment successfully with structure; he had learned to produce symbols that were pointed and useful without being ornate or "arty"; and he had increased his skill in producing images of sharp impressions with the greatest economy of words. He had, in short, established most of the techniques which he would use later.

---

[93] Gelfant, pp. 151-153.

1

U.S.A. (1937) has been variously interpreted as exemplifying the Marxist and Anarchist philosophies as well as the teachings of Veblen and Gibbon or combinations of these. The influence of Whitman is also sometimes suggested. Actually, this work partakes of all of the "isms" and philosophies suggested above because the author himself probably had not consciously subscribed to one viewpoint to the exclusion of all others. In one sense, the work is the gathering of materials on which to base an opinion. In another sense, Dos Passos is here tracing the development in the Twentieth Century of the peculiar set of economic and social institutions or "machines" which arose in this country between the end of the Civil War and the turn of the century; it is the harvest of what was planted in the Gilded Age that he is here recording. In following the development of these institutions, Dos Passos is particularly interested in the relation of man as an individual to the "machines" which are created by the political, economic, and social forces of his time.

All of the "isms" which might have exerted influence over Dos Passos in the writing of *U.S.A.* have been well documented, and it is possible in almost every case to find such evidence written by the author himself. Speaking of his trip to Russia in the fall of 1928, for instance, he remarks,

Everything I thought and wrote that summer was based upon the notion . . . that the violent phase of the Russian revolution was over, that the drive of communist fanaticism was slackening, that the magnificent energies of the Russian people would soon be set to work on making life worth living.[1]

On the other hand, Dos Passos later has Jay Pignatelli, the central character of *Chosen Country* (1951), plan a book entitled *Decline of the West*, *"only more like Gibbon than Spengler"*.[2] Dos Passos has also produced ample evidence that he was deliberately striving for a neutral viewpoint. He is most prolific in comments which show him to be free from Marxist influence. In *Orient Express* (1927) he worries about the "poor devils" imprisoned by the Checka.[3] In *Journeys Between Wars* (1938) he gives the story of an Englishman he met in Russia in 1928 and reveals the effect that the man's terror had on him, and when he leaves Russia, he can't "show his face" to the young communists and say that he stands with them. Later he recalls that he had fallen into a real fear that he would not be allowed to leave Russia.[4] He also indicates that he hated the classification of Marxist "the way the devil hates holy water",[5] and that as early as 1926 he felt there had already been too many "phrases, badges, opinions, banners, imported from Russia" and other places.[6]

The characters in *U.S.A.*, then, are individuals subjected to the pressures of their environment, not propaganda puppets. If they accept the conditions of the "machine" as does J. Ward Moorehouse and rise to economic success while losing their souls or if, like Eveline Hutchins, they seek escape in sex and in artistic and political dilettantism, it is because, being what they are, they choose it or they are driven to it. The three volumes comprising

---

[1] John Dos Passos, *The Theme is Freedom* (New York, Dodd, Mead & Company, 1956), p. 59.

[2] John Dos Passos, *Chosen Country* (Boston, Houghton Mifflin Company, 1951), p. 422.

[3] John Dos Passos, *Orient Express* (New York, Harper & Brothers, 1927), pp. 45 and 48.

[4] John Dos Passos, *Journeys Between Wars* (New York, Harcourt, Brace and Company, 1938), pp. 239 and 247. *See also The Theme is Freedom*, p. 66.

[5] *The Theme is Freedom*, p. 7.

[6] *Ibid.*, p. 8. For further comments by Dos Passos on his attempt to be neutral, *see* also his "Reminiscence of a Middle-Class Radical", *National Review*, I (January 18, 1956), pp. 9-11.

U.S.A. trace the progress of the relation of man to his "machines" from the end of the nineteenth century to the stock market crash at the end of 1929. The study includes the whole of the social, political, and economic system of the United States. The means of evaluating the "machines" is the study of the lives of the individuals who are moulded by them, who are subjected to their pressures, and who sometimes rebel against them.

2

J. Ward Moorehouse, an acid portrait of the American business-man as he is viewed by everyone except the American business-man, begins his Horatio Algeresque rise to wealth in the public schools by "getting considerable fame one term by a corner in agates . . .".[7] Years later, when he is forced to leave college be-cause of financial difficulties, he goes to work in a real estate office. At that time, he is awash with sentimentality, his mind dwelling on three things: the "Strenuous Life", "a lovely girl to fall in love with him", and his desire to be a song writer.[8] While working for the Ocean City Improvement and Realty Company, he meets Annabelle Marie Strang, the daughter of a socially prominent and wealthy throat specialist. After she carefully ar-ranges for him to seduce her, he thinks, "Now she'll have to marry me." [9] Later, when he discovers that she has been unfaithful to him all along, Moorehouse's reaction follows the pattern of com-promise that reveals his desire to "get ahead" at all costs:

For a while he thought he'd go down to the station and take the first train out and throw the whole business to ballyhack, but there was the booklet to get out, and there was a chance that if the boom did come he might get in on the ground floor, and his connection with money and the Strangs; opportunity knocks but once at a young man's door. . . .

[7] John Dos Passos, *The 42nd Parallel, U.S.A.* (New York, The Modern Library, 1937), p. 175. Unless otherwise indicated all subsequent references to *The 42nd Parallel, Nineteen Nineteen*, and *The Big Money* are from the Modern Library edition of *U.S.A.*

[8] *Ibid.*, p. 178.

[9] *Ibid.*, p. 191.

When he went up to Philadelphia the next time he read proof on the booklet. . . .

He also took up a draft of the wedding invitations to be engraved. . . .[10]

Moorehouse's whole life turns more and more to the accumulation of money and prestige. When Annabelle's behavior leads him to sue for divorce, he writes her,

I now understand why you prefer the company of foreigners, bohemians and such to that of ambitious young Americans.

I have no desire to cause you or your father any pain or publicity, but in the first place you must refrain from degrading the name of Moorehouse while you still legally bear it and also I feel that when the divorce is satisfactorily arranged I shall be entitled to some compensation for the loss of time, etc., and the injury to my career that has come through your fault.[11]

Moorehouse is working for a steel company in Pittsburg during the Homestead strike, and his reaction to it indicates not only where his sympathies lie, but also how he has learned to take advantage of events to promote himself:

. . . there were strikers killed by the mine guards and certain writers from New York and Chicago who were sentimentalists began to take a good deal of space in the press with articles flaying the steel industry and the feudal conditions in Pittsburg as they called them . . . Ward said that what was necessary was an entirely new line in the publicity of the industry to educate the public by carefully planned publicity extending over a term of years. . . . he felt he ought to be at the head of it because he was just wasting his time at the Bessemer products. . . . He talked of going to Chicago and starting an advertising agency of his own. Mr. McGill smiled and stroked his steelgray mustache and said, "Not so fast, young man; you stay around here a while yet and on my honor you won't regret it," and Ward said that he was willing, but here he'd been in Pittsburgh five years and where was he getting?[12]

The result is that an information bureau is founded and Ward is put in charge with a salary of $10,000 per year. Later, after Moorehouse inaugurates his own firm as Public Relations Counsel, he is soon busy

[10] *Ibid.*, p. 193.
[11] *Ibid.*, p. 205.
[12] *Ibid.*, pp. 255-256.

keeping the public informed about the state of relations between capital and labor and stemming the propaganda of the sentimentalists and reformers, upholding American ideas against crazy German socialistic ideas and the panaceas of discontented dirtfarmers in the Northwest.[13]

In short, he has become the spokesman for the "machine". After the war, his establishment at the Peace Conference is a part of his work as representative for big business:

For the Peace Conference, J. W. had a suite at the Crillon, with his blonde secretary Miss Williams at a desk in a little anteroom, and Morton his English valet serving tea in the late afternoon.[14]

He has endless conversations with a Mr. Rasmussen of Standard Oil concerning the struggle between the United States and England for "protectorates" over lands rich in oil resources, and Rasmussen labels Moorehouse, "the key to the key men". Moorehouse comments to Eveline once, when his actual cynicism is allowed to come to the surface, on what he thinks he could do for American interests at the Peace Conference:

"The President is surrounded by sinister intrigues, why, even the presidents of the great corporations don't realize that now is the time to spend money, to spend it like water. I could have the French press in my pocket in a week with the proper resources, even in England I have a hunch that something could be done if it was handled in the right way. And then the people are fully behind us everywhere, they are sick of autocracy and secret diplomacy, they are ready to greet American democracy, American democratic business methods with open arms. The only way for us to secure the benefits of the peace to the world is for us to dominate it. Mr. Wilson doesn't realize the power of a modern campaign of scientific publicity. . . ." [15]

At this point Moorehouse is so sure of himself and so completely enamored of the "machine" that he is totally unaware of the ironic quality of his unconscious indictment of it. But despite the difficulties he encounters, Moorehouse is able to report to the press that

an accord, a working agreement had been reached between certain American oil producers and perhaps the Royal Dutch-Shell, oh, no,

[13] *Ibid.*, p. 282.
[14] *Nineteen Nineteen*, p. 295.
[15] *Ibid.*, pp. 312-313.

of course not to set the prices but a proof of a new era of international cooperation that was dawning in which great aggregations of capital would work together for peace and democracy, against reactionaries and militarists on the one hand and against the bloody forces of bolshevism on the other.[16]

After the war, Moorehouse returns to the United States where his chronicle is completed on the eve of the Stock Market crash as he directs the strategy for the firm's acquisition of the Bingham patent medicine account and then launches an attack against the passage of pure food and drug acts which would hurt his client's business.

Eleanor Stoddard's life is a long parasitic search for security in which, while she is perhaps unconscious of the "machine" as such, she carefully conforms to its pressures. In her desire to escape the ugly in life, she attaches herself first to one person and then to another until she finally meets Moorehouse. While she is working at Marshall Field's in Chicago she meets a Miss Perkins, who lives in the same apartment house. Their relationship sets a pattern:

She had dinner every evening with Miss Perkins and Miss Perkins thought a great deal of her and bought her clothes and took her with her driving in the park and sometimes to the theater. ... Just how much [money] she had left Eleanor hadn't been able to find out, but as she always took the best seats at the theater and liked going to dinner at expensive hotels and restaurants and hired a carriage by the half day whenever she wanted one, she gathered that she must be well off.[17]

When Miss Perkins dies, Eleanor envisions headlines, "MARSHALL FIELD EMPLOYEE INHERITS MILLION", but she gets only a diamond brooch. When Elanor bursts out crying, the lawyers are moved by her being so "touched by the remembrance of her old friend".[18] She is more successful at the store. She becomes the chief ingredient in a quarrel between two supervisors, and she is careful to pick the winning side, so that she becomes known as "teacher's pet" and gets a raise and a big commission.[19] Always

---

[16] *Ibid.*, pp. 463-464.
[17] *The 42nd Parallel*, p. 227.
[18] *Ibid.*, pp. 229-231.
[19] *Ibid.*, p. 228.

keeping her relations with men on the "platonic" level, Eleanor
soon finds Tom Curtis,

who was an elderly redfaced man, fond of music and chorus girls and
drinking, who belonged to all the clubs. ... He had a box at the
opera. ... He claimed to be thoroughly sick of social life and enjoyed
taking an interest in the ... decorating business. He kept in close
touch with Wall Street and would occasionally turn over to Eleanor
a couple of shares that he was trading in. If they rose it was her gain,
if they fell it was his loss. ... Sometimes he was a little too affec-
tionate coming home in a taxicab ... but Eleanor would scold him
and he'd be very contrite the next day, and send her great boxes of
white flowers.[20]

After Eleanor goes to New York and meets Moorehouse, she
follows the same pattern of taking without giving. When Moorehouse comes to see her once to pour out his problems, Eleanor
gives him no encouragement, but when he leaves she immediately
begins to worry about her unpaid bills:

She'd counted on the thousand dollar's worth of shares J. W. had said
would be hers if he made the killing he expected in that Venezuela
Oil stock. Something must have gone wrong or else he would have
spoken of it.[21]

His preoccupation and his attempts to confide in her never make
a dent in her consciousness. The only time she ever lends herself
to Moorehouse as anything more than a decoration is after he
has been seduced by Eveline. Eleanor does not otherwise de-
scend to the common vulgarities of life nor does she relinquish
her hold on Moorehouse until well after the war; then she merely
abandons a dying man in order to leach on to the security offered
by a Russian prince.

Eveline Hutchins is probably the least comprehending of the
victims of the "machine". She early develops an artistic talent and
a passion for the poetry and art of the Pre-Raphaelite Brother-
hood. She becomes more and more obsessed with sex and
finally achieves such an identification between art and sex that
her posing nude for an artist and her ultimate seduction by him

[20] *Ibid.*, p. 236.
[21] *Ibid.*, p. 354.

are matters of course. She becomes mildly interested in radical politics through her love affair with Don Stevens and briefly becomes interested in Moorehouse. When it becomes obvious to her that no permanent attachment can be made to Moorehouse, she begins to feel adrift in a world too complex for her to cope with. Her solution is to marry bashful, innocent, young Paul Johnson. They return to the United States, and she quickly relegates him to the status of chief dish washer and begins to collect another group of lovers, including Charley Anderson. Paul finally divorces her, and she begins an affair with a poet, but her chaotic attempts to find happiness and to escape the pressures of life can end only in suicide. Mary French, who sees Eveline a few days before that event, sums up Eveline's career: "Their silly life tells on them." [22]

Janey Williams, like Moorehouse, assumes that this is the best of all possible worlds, nations, economic systems. Her reward for this assumption and for her diligent service to the "machine" as personified by J. Ward Moorehouse is a continual narrowing of viewpoint, a continual narrowing of interests, until she becomes scarcely more than an appendage of her employer, scarcely more useful to society than her typewriter. When the war hysteria becomes widespread, she gives up her job because her employer at that time is a German. She remains unmoved by her brother's denunciation of the war:

"The whole damn war's crooked from start to finish. Why don't they torpedo any French Line boasts? Because the Frogs have it all set with the Jerries, see, that if the Jerries leave their boats alone they won't shell the German factories back of the front. . . . I'm tellin' ye, Janey, this war's crooked, like every other goddam thing." [23]

Rather, she contemplates telling Moorehouse, who is by then her employer, that another of his secretaries is Pro-German because the girl suggests that a group of French officers on a military mission are loafers and "she'd rather see a mission of private soldiers". [24]

[22] *The Big Money*, p. 550.
[23] *The 42nd Parallel*, pp. 344-345.
[24] *Ibid.*, pp. 345-346.

Once under the domination of the "machine", Janey becomes increasingly aware of social caste, and she begins unconsciously to reject her brother Joe. Once, for example, she will not let him come to her apartment for fear that he will embarrass her before her friends. She finally reaches the stage of resenting any interruptions of ordinary office routine, and her position in the office becomes so much an extension of the personality of Moorehouse that Dick Savage hides his drinking from her as carefully as he does from Moorehouse.

Joe Williams is also a victim of the "machine", but his life as a sailor and his acquaintances with many different people give him some idea of reality. If his ideas are not comprehensive, they at least explain the world to his satisfaction. During the war, his bitterness towards the "interests" is heightened by his sister's gradually increasing coolness towards him as she moves up the social ladder through her job with Moorehouse, and by his wife's running around with army officers because he won't stay home and get a high-paying job in a munitions factory. His complete mistrust of all politics is shown in his discussion of the war with two I.W.W. men who tell him that the way to prevent war is for the workers to stop making munitions.

Joe said they were goddam right but look at the big money you made. The guys from Chicago said .... that if the working stiffs made a few easy dollars it meant that the war profiteers were making easy millions. They said the Russians had the right idea, make a revolution and shoot the goddam profiteers. ...

They drank another round and Joe said it was all true but what the hell could you do about it? The guys said what you could do about it was join the I.W.W. and carry a red card and be a classconscious worker. Joe said that stuff was only for foreigners, but if somebody started a white man's party to fight the profiteers and the goddam bankers he'd be with 'em.[25]

A short time later another man offers Joe a job listening for just such expressions against the war. Joe's answer to the man also contains his answer to all of the problems he encounters in his life: "Hell, I'm goin' to sea and get out of all this s - - t." [26]

[25] *Nineteen Nineteen*, pp. 170-171.
[26] *Ibid.*, p. 174.

Although Joe's presence embarrasses her, Janey loves him and writes him frequently and finally makes a convert of him:

Joe began to think that maybe she was right. Anyway if you believed the papers the heinies were getting licked, and it was a big opportunity for a young guy if you didn't get in wrong by being taken for a pro-German or a Bolshevik or some goddam thing. After all as Janey kept writing civilization had to be saved and it was up to us to do it. Joe started a savings account and bought him a Liberty bond.[27]

Whether Joe ever seizes his "big opportunity" remains in doubt. His last appearance in the trilogy occurs on the night following the Armistice. He is being smashed over the head with a bottle during a celebration.

Richard Ellsworth Savage begins as an idealist. When he first becomes conscious of the horrors of war, he reacts violently and in the manner of Martin Howe in *One Man's Initiation-1917*:

"It's a hell of a note when you have to be ashamed of belonging to your own race. But I swear I am, I swear I'm ashamed of being a man ... it will take some huge wave of hope like a revolution to make me feel any self-respect ever again. ... God, we're a lousy cruel vicious dumb type of tailless ape." [28]

Working as an ambulance driver for the Red Cross, Savage finally has an opportunity to test the courage of his convictions when he is informed that, because of his pacifist sentiments, his services are no longer required.

Dick said he felt he ought to explain his position, and that if the Red Cross felt he hadn't done his duty they ought to give him a courtmartial, he said he felt there were many men in his position who had pacifist views but that the country was at war and now they were willing to do any kind of work they could do to help, but that didn't mean he believed in the war ... Dick kept saying, he ought to be allowed to explain his position, and the major kept saying the incident was closed.[29]

He finally goes to an official very high up in the Red Cross who tells him, "Don't monkey with the buzzsaw", and then to an In-

[27] *Ibid.*, p. 237.
[28] *Ibid.*, p. 190.
[29] *Ibid.*, pp. 207-208.

telligence Officer who loses his temper and bawls Dick out. Dick gives up in disgust and goes home. His immediate reaction is to think:

By gum, he must write some verse: what people needed was stirring poems to nerve them for revolt against their cannibal governments.[30]

Instead, he goes home and gets a commission in the army which he recognizes as his surrender to the pressure of the "machine". His feeling of guilt makes him try to establish his independence by writing a long sarcastic letter in doggerel verse about his gaining the commission, but when a major on the boat begins to take an interest in him, he flushes the letter down the toilet, and with it the last shreds of his independence. Later, when he hears that another pacifist has been given a jail sentence for refusing to register for the draft, he echoes the Red Cross official, "Well", he says, "that comes of monkeying with the buzzsaw". Becoming attached to the Moorehouse entourage in France, he refuses to marry Anne Elizabeth Trent after Eleanor Stoddard suggests that it might be "unsuitable" and thereby dramatizes his moral debility which has resulted from his capitulation to the pressures of the "machine". After the war, Savage learns to smile when Moorehouse smiles and to compete with other vice-presidents for those smiles. After landing the important Bingham patent medicine account, he concludes a drunken celebration in the company of two Negro homosexuals, thus achieving his low water mark in moral degradation just as he reaches the highest material point in his life.

Anne Elizabeth Trent is a middle class girl with the proper instincts who gets her education in social consciousness from her boyfriends while she is in college. Webb, the more radical of the two, encourages her to help picket during strikes and to identify herself with the working class, but when the police arrive, it is Webb who runs away ingloriously, and Anne Elizabeth who is beaten and taken to jail although Webb's avenue of escape was open to her also. Her work with the Near East Relief, while it is partially designed to help her over her brother's death, also in-

---

[30] *Ibid.*, p. 211.

dicates her desire to be of some use in the world, but she soon begins to feel hemmed in by the "Methodist Board of Temperance and Public Morals", as she terms the organization. Her primary relation to the "machine" is that of victim because Dick Savage's cynical treatment of her is purely the result of his fear of ruining his chances with Moorehouse.

Charley Anderson's acceptance of the domination of the "machine" is as unconscious as that of Moorehouse, but Anderson is destroyed by the "machine" because he lacks the finesse to manipulate it for his own ends. He begins his career by getting his education in the labor movement, joining the A. F. of L. and participating in an I. W. W. strike.

After the war, when he goes into business, it soon becomes apparent that through his drinking, Anderson is his own worst enemy. But the drinking is merely symptomatic of more basic problems. The world of the "big money" is alien to Charley Anderson; he cannot live under the pressure of it without steeping himself in seas of whiskey, becoming a ready victim in such condition of the financial manipulators and sharp land promoters. He is drunk during every major business and personal crisis of his life, as when, for example, he trades away the stock in his own company and goes to work for his old competitors, a "sell-out" on his old friend Joe Askew. A staunch supporter of the laboring man in his early days, Anderson now forgets his own origin and tells his friend Bill Cermak the company's plans for handling labor problems:

We're goin' to fire the whole outfit. ... Hell, if they don't like it workin' for us let 'em try to like it workin' for somebody else. ... This is a free country. I wouldn't want to keep a man against his will.[31]

Earlier he had told Bill, "Hell, I ain't no boss. ... I belong with the mechanics. ..." [32] This reversal is purely the result of Charley's insatiable desire for more and more money. Soon he is in a vicious circle, feeling more and more the pressure of the need for money, which drives him to drink, which causes him to lose

[31] *The Big Money*, p. 311.
[32] *Ibid.*, p. 229.

money, etc. Charley is drunk when he allows himself to be financially destroyed – he is also drunk when he symbolically gets in the way of a fast moving train.

Margo Dowling, like Eleanor Stoddard, is a parasite; but, unlike Eleanor, Margo renders a personal service to her gentlemen friends. She is also able to achieve success in Hollywood as an actress, another parasite profession. Although she spends a number of her formative years in a convent, Margo quickly learns to consider every problem in her life from purely social and economic viewpoints. Thus, after a bad beginning with her Cuban husband, she is quick to take advantage of the security offered her by Charley Anderson:

Mr. A, as she called him, kept offering to set Margo up in an apartment on Park Avenue, but she always said nothing doing, what did he think she was, a kept woman? She did let him play the stockmarket a little for her, and buy her clothes and jewelry and take her to Atlantic City and Long Beach weekends.[33]

When Charley takes her to Florida with him after he is financially ruined, she tries to make him rest and stop drinking – appearing to have a genuine concern for his welfare, but just before the operation from which he does not recover, she appears with a blank check in hand. After Charley dies and she is again left penniless, Margo goes to Hollywood where she instinctively goes through the motions of making a good impression. She buys a Rolls-Royce and makes her husband wear a uniform whenever he drives her anywhere. She is finally "discovered" and again shows her native grasp of business by insisteing that the studio lawyers work out the contract with her step-mother:

"Do you mind if I ask my companion Mrs. Mandeville to come around? I'm so ignorant about these things." Then she called up Agnes and they fiddled around talking about the weather until Agnes got there.

Agnes was wonderful. She talked about commitments and important business to be transacted and an estate to care for, and said that at that figure it would not be worth Miss Dowling's while to give up her world cruise, would it darling. . . .[34]

[33] *Ibid.*, p. 327.
[34] *Ibid.*, pp. 403-404.

After a series of "appearances" and seductions, and after the death of her husband, Margo assures her success by marrying the director who discovers her.

Fenian McCreary's sympathies lie wholly with the laboring class, especially with members of the I. W. W. which he joins as a young man not long after reading the sentence in his socialist uncle's printing shop, "It is time for all honest men to band together to resist the ravages of greedy privilege." [35] At first Mac's devotion to this "cause" is sufficient to make him leave the girl he is engaged to in order to go help a strike. The girl writes that she is pregnant, and while Mac listens to Bill Haywood speak to the miners, he decides he must go back and marry the girl, wondering the while "what Big Bill would do if he'd got a girl in trouble like that".[36] After they have been married a while, Mac's wife begins to compare his low wages with those of her brothers and to object to his "wobbly" interests. One day when he sees a young man being beaten by two policemen for reading the Declaration of Independence on a street corner, the comparison of his own tameness with the determination of the young man brings home the realization, "I guess I've sold out to the sonsobitches allright, allright." [37] When his home life finally becomes unbearable, he walks out. His moment of regret is followed by a type of exultation:

"Well, I'm through," he said aloud as if he were speaking to somebody else. Then only did the thought come to him, "I'm free to see the country now, to work for the movement, to go on the bum again." [38]

But Mac's captivity has been too much for him. Arriving in Mexico where he plans to join Zapata, he sets up housekeeping all over again, actually achieving a higher place on the social ladder than he had occupied in the United States. When he flees Mexico City during a revolution, he thinks only momentarily of returning to the United States. He has too much capital in Mexico.

[35] *The 42nd Parallel*, p. 19.
[36] *Ibid.*, p. 102.
[37] *Ibid.*, pp. 114-115.
[38] *Ibid.*, p. 123.

Mary French is closely tied to the communists, but unlike most of Dos Passos' communists, she spends little time discussing radical doctrine. Her primary concern is her work in the labor movement. In this capacity she is bitterly opposed to the "machine" and the status quo. It is her desire to belong completely to the people she trys to help, and she throws herself into her work with such zeal that she is perpetually on the verge of collapse. After having worked with G. H. Barrow for some time, she sees through his activities and yells, "We're just laborfakers." [39] She next joins the Sacco and Vanzetti defense committee and works tirelessly, haunted always by the spectre of their electrocution. Having been arrested and beaten by the police herself, she encounters Barrow again, who begins to talk about wanting to help. When she suggests that he might allow himself to be arrested for the sake of a demonstration, he begins talking himself out of it, but she cuts him off angrily, "I didn't think you'd take the risk." [40] Once when Mary is near exhaustion, her friend Ada Cohn takes her to one of Eveline's parties. Mary indignantly renews her quarrel with the "machine":

"It's a waste," Mary cried out savagely. Suddenly able to articulate. ... "The food they waste and the money they waste while our people starve in tarpaper barracks."

And she adds,

"I'm sick of this parasite life. I'm going back to the office tomorrow. ... I've got to call up tonight to see if they got in all right with that load of condensed milk." [41]

Then she goes back to the labor movement.

Ben Compton early becomes known as a "socialist agitator". His movement to the political left provides him with a beating while he is with the I. W. W. and gets him arrested for making seditious statements in a speech to the communists. The court offers to drop the charges, but Ben retorts, "If you let me out, I'll do my best to oppose capitalist war until you arrest me

[39] *Ibid.*, p. 146.
[40] *Ibid.*, p. 454.
[41] *Ibid.*, p. 556.

again." [42] Like Andrews in *Three Soldiers*, he seems determined to make the "machine" destroy him. After he is released from his term in jail, Ben throws himself back into party work, leading strikes and making speeches, but he is finally expelled from the party. He tells Mary French,

"I've been expelled from the party . . . oppositionist . . . exceptionalism . . . a lot of nonsense . . . Well, that doesn't matter, I'm still a revolutionist . . . I'll continue to work outside of the party.

But when he asks her to help him get into relief work where "the discipline isn't so strict", she tells him, "I don't think they want any disrupting influences in the I. L. D." [43] In this manner Ben is abandoned by the "machine" to which he has given his life.

Thus, in the three novels comprising *U.S.A.*, Dos Passos again uses a structural pattern based on the characters' awareness of reality. Richard Elsworth Savage and John Ward Moorehouse, for example, both come to full consciousness of reality, and both make the deliberate choice of surrendering to the "machine". Moorehouse, reared in the quintessence of Nineteenth Century political and economic conservatism, believes nobly and sentimentally in the system as it is, and when he first encounters the shoddiness of it in Annabelle Marie Strang, his hesitation is only momentary. He marries her despite her falseness, and his reasons for so doing are imminently practical; after that choice, he never again hesitates. Richard Savage, on the other hand, has a better comprehension of the "machine" before he is forced to choose. His experience in the Ambulance Corps provides him with a great deal of evidence on which to base an intelligent decision; yet when the moment of choice comes, he flushes his poem and his conscience down the drain together, and it is because of his comprehension of the depravity of his choice that Dos Passos provides for him complete degradation. These two men and Margo Dowling, corrupt though they be, are the only genuine realists in the book. The other characters are idealistic romantics like Ben Compton who simply refuse to acknowledge reality; some, like Eveline Hutchins and Joe Wiliams, are merely victims of a mechanistic

[42] *Nineteen Nineteen*, p. 446.
[43] *The Big Money*, pp. 539-540.

determinism which they do not even understand. Mary French understands and consciously rejects the "machine" which supports her worthless mother, but in her efforts to destroy it, she does not see what the Communist Party – another "machine" – has done to her.

3

Most of the structural devices of *U.S.A.* are the result of the author's previous experimentation. Devices present in *Three Soldiers* and *Manhattan Transfer* are used again in the trilogy, but the basic plan was derived from *Rosinante to the Road Again*. In that book the episodes of narrative fiction alternate with essays and travel narrative relative to the theme. All of the narrative fiction episodes are given the same title, "Talk by the Road", and they are all carried forward with a great deal of belabored symbolism. It is interesting to note that *Journeys Between Wars* (1938), which contains nearly all of the material in *Rosinante to the Road Again* and *Orient Express* (1927) in addition to other material not previously published in book form, shows a marked improvement in structural arrangement when compared with the earlier material. While some of the new material is rather chaotic, the sections containing the materials from the two previously published books are greatly streamlined and much of the symbolic paraphernalia is omitted.

But in *U.S.A.* the division of the background material into "Camera Eye", "Biography", and "Newsreel" sections is merely external framework. The real artistry of Dos Passos is in his careful arrangement of the parts of the novels so as to maintain a unity of impression and a consciousness of the breadth of view which the author undertakes. It is this careful planning that produces the progression in *The Big Money* of the biography of Veblen being followed by the narrative of Mary French whose mother inherits some stock and settles down to a life of clipping coupons while Mary, visiting her mother, uses her temporary leisure to read *The Theory of the Leisure Class*. Another example of such

structuring is the arrangement of Mac's story in *The 42nd Parallel.*
There is a space of nearly 200 pages between Mac's arrival in
Mexico and the next narrative episode devoted to him, but nearly
every "Newsreel" in the intervening space carries some reference
to the revolutionary movement in Mexico.

Structure is also used to help develop theme through the organization of the materials within each of the three books of the trilogy.
In *The 42nd Parallel* Dos Passos covers the history of the nation
from 1900 to 1917, tracing the rise of big business and economic
imperialism through the "Biographies" and "Newsreels" and using
the fictional lives of his characters as a means of demonstrating the
effects of these conditions on the individual. All major devices
carry the theme of the social, economic, and political organization of a nation that is in the process of separating the upper and
lower classes by an ever widening gulf. The "Biographies" re-
count the lives and works of such benefactors of mankind as
Burbank, Edison, and Steinmetz. Steinmetz is reported to have
been purchased by General Electric in 1892 along with other
"valuable apparatus" from Rudolph Eichemeyer. Andrew Carne-
gie, introduced under the title, "Prince of Peace", is a sample of
those who profited by the advance in technology and who "except
in time of war", liked to endow institutions "to promote universal
peace". Minor C. Keith typifies the economic imperialism ram-
pant at the turn of the century that led to the necessity of protect-
ing American investments abroad and made war an instrument of
foreign policy. Debs, Haywood, Bryan, and La Folette are presented as individuals who struggled with varying degrees of insight
and effectiveness to change the course of American economic,
social, and political growth. The "Camara Eye" sections, a little
like Wordsworth's *Prelude,* focus on the growing consciousness of
the writer, and in them, Dos Passos records an increasing awareness of the social and economic problems besetting the nation.
They range from a description of an encounter with a young bum
to the disgusted rejection of the cold culture of Harvard. Through
the "Newsreels", Dos Passos is able to touch on all phases of his
theme. Almost half of the "Newsreels" in *The 42nd Parallel* contain at least one item relevant to the class struggle, about one-

third of them contain items which serve to point up the over-whelming separation of the two extremes of the social and eco-nomic ladder, and about one-fifth of them contain indices of the accumulation of political power by the upper classes illustrated by an economic interest in wars, revolutions, and internal troubles of foreign countries.

In *Nineteen Nineteen*, Dos Passos focuses his attention on the two wars – one being fought by men like Joe Williams and the other by men like Lieutenant Savage – and on the peace con-ference which followed and which was too concerned with the interests represented by Moorehouse and too negligent of the Fourteen Points. Once again the four major elements of the novel are brilliantly articulated. The "Camera Eye" sections present a steady progression of impressions from war, to the Armistice, to the consciousness of such radical philosophies as anarchism and communism. The "Newsreels" follow approximately the same pattern but reveal more emotion over Bolshevism and contain references to the economics of war and peace. Among the "Bio-graphies" are those of Theodore Roosevelt, the imperialist for whom Dos Passos shows a grudging admiration; J. P. Morgan, whom Dos Passos would list as one of the major causes for Amer-ica's entry into the war; and Woodrow Wilson, who began by promising "neutrality in thought and deed" and who ended by pursuing the policy of "force without stint or limit, force to the utmost". Opposed to these three there are Randolph Bourne, one of the first to see through Wilson's "betrayal"; Paxton Hibbin, a man who really tried to make it a "war to end war" because he believed in the new world; and Jack Reed, the tireless worker who virtually killed himself trying to make the Declaration of Independence come true. There are Joe Hill and Wesley Everest, two I. W. W. men whose martyrdom suggests the loss of liberty in the United States as well as in Europe; and finally, there is the Unknown Soldier who, Dos Passos suggests, gave his life and his identity for the protection of Morgan investments and for a peace that could not endure because it was based upon nationalism and greed rather than upon the Fourteen Points, and to whom "Wood-row Wilson brought a bouquet of poppies".

The Big Money, which covers the years 1920 to 1929, is the chronicle of America's failure in the post-war period. That failure is presented through the unabashed pursuit of wealth, prestige, and power at the expense of political freedom, equality of economic opportunity, and human dignity. As in the first two volumes, the biographies are those of men whose lives or work shaped the age by their contributions to it and who helped to initiate industries that resulted in the amassing of great fortunes. There are Hearst and Insull, whose wealth and power were derived at second hand. There is the picture of Veblen whose books went so far toward explaining the social and economic jungle around him, and there are Rudolph Valentino and Isadora Duncan who contributed nothing of value and who so ably personified the cultural absurdity of the age. The remainder of the national background, traced in the "Newsreels" is a chaos of items showing the reckless pursuit of love, beauty, and adventure – methods of escaping the pressures of the age; the constantly growing concern with strikes, radicals, and political upheaval; and the steadily increasing roar of the business boom leading up to the depression. The "Camera Eye" sections show a gradually increasing interest in the conflict between the "haves" and the "have-nots" until a high pitch of intensity is reached in numbers forty-nine and fifty, both of which deal with Sacco and Vanzetti. The first pertains to the years preceeding the executions when Dos Passos worked on the defense committee, and the second follows immediately after a "Newsreel" containing the headline, "SACCO AND VANZETTI MUST DIE". These two "Camera Eye" sections are of central importance to the theme of *The Big Money* because Sacco and Vanzetti are human personifications of the failure which Dos Passos illustrates through the lives of his fictional characters. They are the ultimate victims. In *Facing the Chair*, Dos Passos had written, "If they die what little faith many millions of men have in the chance of Justice in this country will die with them." [44] In the last "Camera Eye" dealing with

---

[44] John Dos Passos, *Facing the Chair; Story of the Americanization of Two Foreignborn Workmen* (Boston, Sacco-Vanzetti Defense Committee, 1927), p. 127.

Sacco and Vanzetti, he writes, "all right we are two nations", and then concludes, "we stand defeated America".[45]

The author's technical skills are at a high standard throughout the three volumes of *U.S.A.*, and while there is considerable divergence of opinion concerning his ability to create character,[46] it is certain that the slightest character who appears in *U.S.A.* has more vitality and speaks with a far more natural language per inch of narrative than any half-dozen other characters he had created previously. The important point is not how they compare with characters created by Faulkner or Hemingway, but how well they serve Dos Passos' needs within the structure of the kind of novel he was writing. From that viewpoint, the characters in *U.S.A.* are probably the best group ever created by Dos Passos. The following conversation between Eveline Hutchins and Janey Williams illustrates both character and conflict:

"Busy as ever, Miss Williams," she said.
"It's better to be busy," she said. "It keeps a person out of mischief. ... It seems to me that in Paris they waste a great deal of time. ... I never imagined that there could be a place where people could sit around so much of the time."
"The French value their leisure more than anything."
"Leisure's all right if you have something to do with it. ... but this social life wastes so much of our time. ... People come to lunch and stay all afternoon, I don't know what we can do about it. ... it makes a very difficult situation." Miss Williams looked hard at Eveline. "I don't suppose you have much to do at the Red Cross anymore, do you, Miss Hutchins?"
Eveline smiled sweetly. "No, we just live for our leisure like the French." [47]

Dos Passos also uses the dream-sequence in *U.S.A.*, although not as frequently as in previous novels. For example, during her work on the Sacco-Vanzetti defense committee, Mary French continues her impossible labors in her dreams:

... she was trying to glue a broken teapot together and as soon as

---

[45] *The Big Money*, pp. 462 and 464.
[46] *Cf.* James T. Farrell, "Dos Passos and the Critics", *The American Mercury*, XLVII (August, 1939), p. 492 with Granville Hicks, "John Dos Passos", *Bookman*, LXXV (April, 1932), p. 35.
[47] *Nineteen Nineteen*, p. 328.

she got one side of it mended the other side would come to pieces again, she was trying to mend a rent in her skirt and by the time the bottom was sewed the top had come undone again; she was trying to put together pieces of a torn typewritten sheet, the thelegram was of the greatest importance, she couldn't see, it was all a blur before her eyes; it was the evidence that would force a new trial. . . .[48]

The freshness of the images and the economy of words reveal Dos Passos at his best. At Long Beach, for example, "a great blue wind was streaming off the sea blurred by little cool patches of mist".[49] Of Edison, he says, "In Detroit there was a public library and he read it." [50] There are times when the run-together words used by Dos Passos are more mannerism than elements of style, but in *U.S.A.* that technique is used to express patterns of speech, as in "before the worldsfair Beforeyouwereborn",[51] of habits of mind and therefore an aid in characterization, as in Eveline's "Yourfather mustn't be disturbed, and Dearmother's. . . ." [52] or of the machine-like quality of an action as in the passage from Henry Ford's biography: "reach under, adjust washer, screw down bolt, shove in cotterpin, reachunder adjustwasher, screwdown bolt, reachunderadjust screwdownreachunderadjust. . . ." [53]

Dos Passos' fondness for irony is given ample scope in *U.S.A.* with such incidents as the mock-epic battle in which an army officer tries to make a group of pacifists stand up while the orchestra plays the national anthem. The episode concludes:

The woman with the red hat picked up a bowl of lobster mayonnaise and was holding back the crowd by chucking handfuls of it in their faces. At that moment three cops appeared and arrested the damn pacifists. Everybody stood around wiping mayonnaise off his clothes. The band played *The Star Spangled Banner* again and everybody tried to sing it but it didn't make much of an effect because nobody knew the words.[54]

And there is one passage that sounds a great deal like Mark

---

[48] *The Big Money*, pp. 452-453.
[49] *Ibid.*, p. 78.
[50] *The 42nd Parallel*, p. 297.
[51] *Ibid.*, p. 25.
[52] *Nineteen Nineteen*, p. 107.
[53] *The Big Money*, p. 55.
[54] *The 42nd Parallel*, pp. 408-409.

Twain's "nobody hurt . . . killed a nigger" episode in *Huckleberry Finn*:

One night Mother was so frightened on account of all the rifleshots but it was allright turned out to be nothing but a little shooting they'd been only shooting a greaser that was all.[55]

The "Newsreels" and the ordering of the sequence of the various sections within the individual novels give Dos Passos' fine sense of juxtaposition excellent opportunities for irony, humor, and emphasis. Among the runtogether headlines, for example, are such items as the following:

GEORGE SMITH HANGED WITH HIS BROTHER BY
MOB IN KANSAS MARQUIS OF QUEENSBERRY DEAD [56]

and the following:

Beneath a dreamy Chinese moon
Where love is like a haunting tune
PROFESSOR TORTURES RIVAL [57]

The justaposition of the closing words of "Camera Eye (51)" and the title of the "Biography" of Samuel Insull illustrates the effects obtained through the careful ordering of the sequence of the different sections:

he lifts his hand towards the telephone
the deputies crowd in the door
we have only words against
POWER SUPERPOWER [58]

Both the internal and external structure and the writing in *U.S.A.* are of the highest craftsmanship. There is no wasted motion; everything goes to develop theme, to carry the characters forward in their conflict with the "machine". Those who are capable of adjusting to the pressures of it attain material success and lose all spiritual direction in the process; others are crushed by a system which they do not understand or they are destroyed when

[55] *Ibid.*, p. 25.
[56] *Ibid.*, p. 54.
[57] *The Big Money*, p.256. Italics his.
[58] *Ibid.*, p. 525.

they consciously oppose it. One somehow feels the massiveness of Dreiser without being caught in the endless tentacles of detail; and there is also a relief in the abrupt shift from narrative, to "Newsreel" to "Camera Eye" to narrative, to "Biography".

If, in his total picture of the United States, Dos Passos did omit some major human types and leave out almost all reference to the great middle class, he was not, after all, taking the census. However, what he put into *U.S.A.* is as accurate and as vivid a picture of the times as any that can be found in print.

III. *DISTRICT OF COLUMBIA*
THE YEARS OF OUR DEFEAT

1

In *District of Columbia* (1952), his second trilogy, Dos Passos becomes increasingly attentive to the problems of the relation of man to the "machine". In these novels, the "machine" is more often portrayed as a specific organization or group – such as a political party – than as a general institution – such as an economic system. The non-fiction published since 1940 has also generally revealed the same change.

The Adventures of a Young Man (1939), the first book of the trilogy, is the story of the idealist, Glenn Spotswood, who refuses to compromise his ideals and is therefore destroyed by the "machine". His first step toward the "left" results from his association at Columbia University with the liberal Boris Spingarn and Boris' communist wife, Gladys. After graduating, Glenn goes to work in a bank in a small Texas town, but almost immediately he becomes involved in a fight to aid a group of Mexican laborers who have been jailed for going on strike. When Glenn's activities cause him to lose his job, he returns to New York where he becomes active in the Communist Party. Soon he is involved in a communist run miners' strike and is beaten and left for dead by gunmen hired by the mine owners. When he discovers that the party has betrayed its own striking members in order to make them martyrs for the purposes of publicity, Glenn turns on the party with violent public criticism for which he is expelled. Finding himself cut off from further opportunities to help the laborers through the party, Glenn joins the International Brigade to fight facism in Spain, but he finds that even in Spain the Communist Party is the greatest enemy of those it claims to serve. He is imprisoned by the Communists and is freed only when he volunteers for a dangerous assignment. His resulting death is the novel's most pointed comment on the relationship between the idealist and the "machine" which he opposes.

The two parts of the theme divide the book approximately in half. The first part shows how a young man of the "professional class" might gradually become more and more attracted to communism so that he finally becomes an ardent party worker. The second half of the book shows his work for the party, his awakening to the party's destruction of the ideals it preaches and of its own members who are outside of the ruling caste, his attempt to force the party to live up to its ideals, and, finally, his destruction by the party. The theme of the novel is suggested by Dos Passos himself, writing in *The Ground We Stand On* (1941):

The history of the political notions of American intellectuals during the past twenty years is largely a record of how far the fervor of their hopes of a better world could blind them to the realities under their noses. Conversion was followed sooner or later by disillusion. . . .[1]

In *The Adventures of a Young Man*, as in most of Dos Passos' other works, the structure is an outgrowth of the theme. In this case, both phases of the central theme are developed antiphonally by the introduction from time of time of viewpoints contrary to those maintained by Glenn as he progresses through his conversion and disillusionment.

The first incident in the book sets the pattern for the remaining major incidents in Glenn's life. He tries to stop two boys from bullying a third and is himself beaten up for his pains. When a teacher stops the squabble, the boy whom he had tried to help tells the teacher that Glenn was the one who had been bullying him. Later, when the boys want to play "Washington at Valley Forge", he refuses to play the part of Benedict Arnold. One other important episode occurs before Glenn begins to fall under the

[1] John Dos Passos, *The Ground We Stand on: Some Examples from the History of a Political Creed* (New York, Harcourt, Brace and Company, 1941), p. 6.

spell of radical philosophies. When he is working as a counselor at a summer camp, one of the boys misbehaves and causes a gread deal of trouble. The owner of the camp blames Paul Graves, the senior counselor, and fires him. Glenn, feeling at least partially responsible, quits his job because he believes Paul has been treated unjustly. Later, Paul tells him,

"Wasn't any skin off your ass."
  "But it wasn't fair. It was his fault for letting Fats go on the trip."
  "You'd oughta kept your mouth shut." [2]

During his first year in college, Glenn reads Henry George and becomes secretary and treasurer of a "Single Tax Association". He also makes plans to work his way into the Northwest during the following summer to study conditions "among the migratory workers in the harvest fields". He approaches the job and the people in the manner of a condescending social worker, preaching, for example, to the old harvest hand, Ben, about the evils of drink. But the "wobbly" talk he hears and the general conditions he sees make a strong impression on him. When Glenn goes to New York to enter Columbia, he still doesn't know what he is politically, although he begins to fall more and more under the spell of Gladys Spingarn. His gradual movement toward the party is contrasted with the antiphonal comments of the liberals, Boris Spingarn and Mike Gulick. Glenn hears Gladys and Boris arguing:

"Old Russia was hell," Gladys cried out in a tense voice. "Capitalism made life a hell."
  "New Russia has been hell for a great many," said Boris. ... "We haven't been there but we ought to know. Your mother's people were from Odessa, weren't they? My uncle Aaron was there all through it." [3]

And later Boris comments that he believes in the "proletariat at work" but the "proletarian hot air" makes him sick. When Glenn's

[2] John Dos Passos, *The Adventures of a Young Man, District of Columbia* (Boston, Houghton-Mifflin Company, 1952), p. 59. Unless otherwise indicated, all subsequent references to *The Adventures of a Young Man, Number One*, or *The Grand Design* are from this edition of *District of Columbia*.
  [3] *Ibid.*, pp. 113-115.

communist interests cause him to have bad mid-term reports, he goes to ask Mike Gulick's advice about dropping out of school. Mike laughs at Glenn's tirade about the "exploiting class and the producing class" and advises Glenn not to let himself become a "soapbox fanatic". Mike also tells him that "society is based on habits: people's habits could only be changed little by little in the direction of social consciousness".[4]

When Glenn graduates, he is still uncommitted, although all of his sympathies lie on the side of the communists. He visits his father who tells him, ". . . there's a certain selfindulgence in extremism, which I am coming more and more to distrust." [5] The polarity of their views is illustrated in almost the last words they exchange. Glenn says,

". . . only the revolutionary working class, following the lead of the Russian working class, can really give us world peace."

Dad threw down his napkin and started walking to the diningroom door, saying in a low angry voice that preaching violence and hate was a funny way to work for peace. He believed reasonable methods of arbitration were just as much needed to negotiate away the causes of wars between classes as wars between nations.[6]

A visit with his old friend Paul Graves contrasts Glenn's attitude with that of the more practical Paul, who suggests that they let the Russians try out communism for about twenty-five years before coming to any conclusions. Paul also tells Glenn that Glenn's opinions are all "hot air" and that they come from "associating with longhaired men and shorthaired girls up there in Greenwich Village". The discussion finally ends with Paul warning Glenn to put his "preconceived notions" away if he really wants to study the system scientifically.[7] That Glenn could not follow Paul's suggestion and that the "fervor" of his "hopes for a better world" could blind him to the "realities under his nose" becomes very clear in the incident of the Mexican laborers which is, in miniature, the same situation exactly as that which eventually causes Glenn to condemn the party. When Silverstone, a com-

[4] *Ibid.*, pp. 121-122.
[5] *Ibid.*, p. 138.
[6] *Ibid.*, pp. 141-142.
[7] *Ibid.*, pp. 147-149.

munist organizer, comes down to "help" the Mexicans, he begins
by planning a veritable flood of leaflets, but Frankie Perez tells
him, "that his people did not need to be told about exploitation. . . . but they would not allow the trial to be made a demonstration for the Marxist interpretation. . . ." [8] The result is that the
communist leaflets are used anyhow and arouse such a response
among the local citizens that the Mexicans' lawyer, Jed Farrington, and Glenn are forced out of town by the combined forces of
the American Legion, the Ku Klux Klan, and the citizens in
general. The Mexicans remain in jail, and Silverstone is "called
away" on party business.

The Slade County miners' strike is probably based on the
Harlan County, Kentucky, strikes which Dos Passos and others
investigated at the invitation of the Communist Party. In his
articles on the Kentucky strikes, he tells of soup kitchens blown
up, of gunbattles between strikers and company men; and he
states in a linking passage in *The Theme is Freedom*, in which
he reprinted the articles, that he remembers the party "denying
help to men who wouldn't play their game".[9] In the novel, the
"help" that the Party officers extend to the miners is similar to
that with which they had encumbered the Mexican laborers.
After company men provoke violence and a number of the miners
are in jail, Silverstone appears, ready to take charge, but he refuses
legal aid to the miners belonging to a non-communist union. The
leader of the communist miners then rejects the party's aid: "Boys",
he says, "I'm stickin' together. . . . us miners we don't want no
different lawyer from the Sladetown boys. We better stick with
our own folks." [10] Even when the other unions agree to cooperate
with the communist union in the defense of the miners, Silverstone and Elmer Weeks, the two highest ranking communists,
refuse to cooperate. Weeks tells Glenn, "we must keep one thing
in mind. Our function is to educate the American workingclass

---

[8] *Ibid.*, p. 164.
[9] John Dos Passos, *The Theme is Freedom* (New York, Dodd, Mead &
Company, 1956), pp. 75 and 87. *See* also John Dos Passos, *State of the
Nation* (Boston, Houghton-Mifflin Company, 1944), pp. 231-232. Dos Passos had also witnessed similar conditions in the Pennsylvania coal region.
[10] *The Adventures of a Young Man*, p. 231.

in revolutionary Marxism. We are not interested in the fates of individuals." [11] Thus, as a means of illustrating the class struggle, the communists mercilessly seek the destruction of their own men. During the whole of the period before and during the trial, Glenn, once mercilessly beaten and left for dead by mine company gunmen, has opportunity to see the Communist Party leaders using their men for such publicity purposes while the other unions quietly get their men out of jail. Not long after the communist miners are given twenty-year sentences, the Party switches its stand to one of cooperation with all of the other unions for purposes of "boring from within". Glenn's reaction reveals his mounting disgust with Party authority:

Glenn found himself yelling into the phone, "Why the hell, if you'd decided to collaborate with the old unions, couldn't you have decided to collaborate with the Mineworkers in time to get them in on the Slade County trials? Don't you know that if you people had gone around to see Connolly and told him you were going to lay off, he might have influenced the prosecutor not to step on the murder charges? Jesus Christ, we might have gotten those boys out of jail." [12]

Glenn tries to discuss the situation with the Party leaders, but no one will listen to him, so he plans to bring up the case before the plenum, but he is expelled from the party before he can take any such action. After his expulsion, Glenn begins to face some of the "realities" that Dos Passos had mentioned, and he is soon writing newspaper articles against the "complete lack of sincerity of the leadership of the official Communist Party . . .".[13] But Glenn retains his faith in the Russian Revolution, and when Paul Graves comes back from several years' work at a Russian Experiment Station, Glenn eagerly asks him about the Five Year Plan. Paul says, "It'll work if Red Joe has to starve every miserable peasant in the Soviet Union to death to make it work . . ." He also says in a burst of very bad prose that "the New Deal's got the fiveyear plan knocked for a row of red squares as a social experiment . . ." and adds that "the rest of the European dictator-

[11] *Ibid.*, p. 253.
[12] *Ibid.*, p. 273.
[13] *Ibid.*, pp. 292-293 and 294.

ships are comic opera, but there's nothing comic opera about the Soviet Union".[14]

Glenn finally begins to realize that it is not just the American branch of the Party that is opportunistic when he meets Frankie Perez in Spain. Frankie tells him:

"Here several different kinds of war. We fight Franco but also we fight Moscow . . . if you go to the Brigada you must not let them fight us. They want to destroy our collectives. They want to institute dictatorship of secret police just like Franco." [15]

His realization of the party's separation from the masses is completed when he meets Jed Farrington, now a full-blown communist leader, who tells him that as soon as they beat Franco, they will have to "clean out" men like Frankie Perez who are "uncontrollables". "We've cleaned out the worst of 'em already",[16] he adds. Glenn's being jailed is merely the unravelling of a predetermined fate once he has placed himself again in the hands of the Party. He is hardly surprised when they arrest him. He dies because he cares enough for the anti-facist cause to undertake a mission that two communist leaders fear to attempt.

2

Number One (1943) is the second volume of *District of Columbia*. It is structured very much like *The Adventures of a Young Man*, the principal difference being the type of "machine". In *Number One* it is the political machine of Homer T. "Chuck" Crawford, the demagogue from Texarkola, a fictional town whose name suggests the East Texas-Arkansas-Oklahoma Bible Belt reactionary environment in which demagogues have traditionally thrived. The central character is Tyler Spotswood, Glenn's older brother. Tyler is the private secretary of Chuck Crawford who is in the process of elevating himself from the House of Representatives to the United States Senate. In a campaign partially

---

[14] *Ibid.*, pp. 297-299.
[15] *Ibid.*, p. 323.
[16] *Ibid.*, p. 326.

managed by Tyler, Chuck goes through a series of maneuvers that leave nothing to the imagination concerning the process of demagoguery in American political campaigns.

After Chuck is elected, he organizes the Struck Oil Corporation – in which Tyler is a dummy officer – for the purpose of exploiting oil leases in the State Park Bottoms. The corporation also buys stock in Chuck's Every Man a Millionaire Corporation, purchases a radio station for Chuck's political use, and pays him a high salary. Thus he is using public funds to finance his political campaigns and to supplement his own salary. Chuck's career in Washington is more or less unhampered until he begins attacking the administration, which is that of Franklin D. Roosevelt. First there is trouble over seating Chuck's delegates at a party convention, and then his oil company is investigated by the Treasury Department and the Attorney General. Chuck, who manages to avoid conviction himself, arranges for Tyler to take the blame, and Tyler, with only a momentary temptation to turn state's evidence, allows himself to be victimized.

That *Number One*, like a whole group of novels by Dos Passos' contemporaries, was probably at least inspired by the career of Huey P. Long is not the important consideration. Rather, Dos Passos is interested in the demagogue as a political phenomena and in the responses he evokes from idealists like Tyler Spotswood who look to him for leadership, from businessmen like Jerry Evans who want to use him, and from the common people, who vote for him.

Tyler, like his brother, is an idealist. He becomes an enthusiastic worker for Chuck because he believes in the ideals which Chuck preaches. As Tyler gradually comes to realize that Chuck's practices are far removed from his ideals, he becomes disillusioned, but in the end he refuses to testify against Chuck because that would mean following the betrayal pattern of Chuck; instead, he remains loyal on the theory that a man must make himself morally straight before he begins to work on either the body politic or the politicians. Tyler's relation to the "machine" is, like Glenn's, based on idealism and an inadequate comprehension of the real world. Finally each merges his consciousness with reality and sees the "machine" for what it really is, and out of the resulting disillusionment is born the positive individual act which upholds the ideal but which rejects the "machine".

Tyler is already a supporter of Chuck when the story begins. He tells Ed James, Glenn's banking associate turned journalist,

"Why man alive Chuck Crawford was born right out of the middle of the American people ... wait till you meet him ... Of course I told you from the beginning I'm crazy about him ... If I wasn't I wouldn't be here in Washington." [17]

Chuck's apparent love for the American people manifests itself in his economic schemes which are never explained, although his Every Man a Millionaire ideas sound at times not unlike the single tax of Henry George:

"Why should one million people in this country have all the good things of the world while the other hundred an' nineteen million go naked and hongry an' destitute? It's against common sense an' it's against revealed religion. Don't the Bible lay upon us the injunction, Senator, to spread the good things of the land equally among the people of the land? Leviticus 25, verse 23. ... 'The land shall not be sold forever for the land is mine; for ye are strangers on' sojourners with me' ... an' all the rest of that chapter." [18]

Chuck also explains his "country boy" manners to Ed James, who is hired to write Chuck's autobiography – "You write it in the first person, do you hear? ... I do everythin' in the first person" –

"I know Mr. James you think that's all horsin' an' demagogue foolery ... But lemme tell you jess why I do it. Down where we come from there's a lot of pore people don't eat the proper food ... Those folks they listen to what I say because they know I'm their friend ... That's why every time I get a chance I hammer away at turnip greens or pot liquor or sallets ... a lot of those folk'll think if Ole Chuck eats it it may be worth tryin'. ..." [19]

The political campaign, while it is partially managed by Tyler, is under the constant direction of Chuck. The campaign reveals the "machine" in action. There are Scripture-laden speeches, "impromptu" rallies, hilbilly bands, and secret political deals.

[17] *Number One*, p. 5.
[18] *Ibid.*, p. 11.
[19] *Ibid.*, p. 17.

It is partly through Tyler's association with Sue Ann, Chuck's wife, that Tyler begins to see the rottenness of the man he worships. Su Ann's decency and honesty, for example, contrasted with Chuck's drinking bouts and his parties with cabaret girls, makes Tyler begin to see what he might not otherwise have seen. On one ocasion he tells her, "Sue Ann, I feel like a skunk. . . . What I mean is . . . that if you do things too often that make you feel like a skunk then after a while you get to be a skunk." [20] And making excuses to her to cover one of Chuck's parties makes him wish he could "break down and sob like a baby".[21] It is at such a time that Chuck organizes his Struck Oil Corporation and the radio station, which he insists are "as clean as a hound's tooth", planning, at the same time, to divide the stock in his Every Man a Millionaire Corporation "Just like an apple . . . A Big Apple pie." [22] Tyler's growing recognition of Chuck's corruption is further illustrated during the party convention when Tyler has a conversation with Ed James:

"Of course old Chuck's story is," Ed said, "that it's only by sugar-coatin' them with a certain amount of tomfoolery that he can get over the wholesome truths to Mr. and Mrs. John Citizen . . . Isn't that about the size of it, Toby?"

Tyler nodded. "After all somebody's got to explain the possibilities of the modern setup to the people in words of one syllable. Abe Lincoln did the same thing in his day," he rattled on, feeling his words empty as a parrot's.[23]

This is a far cry from the enthusiastic testimonial he gives Ed James earlier. Tyler's disillusionment turns into rejection during the course of the convention, and he finally tells Sue Ann that he is through and that he is going to leave Chuck.

When Tyler comes back to testify during the investigation of Chuck's quasi-legal corporations, Chuck callously works on Tyler's loyalty in an effort to insure that Tyler will not testify against him. Tyler tries to give noncommital testimony at the hearing and is indicted by the prosecutor who hopes to force him to testify against

[20] *Ibid.*, p. 125.
[21] *Ibid.*, p. 126.
[22] *Ibid.*, p. 139.
[23] *Ibid.*, pp. 152-153.

Chuck. It is the letter that Tyler receives from Glenn that leads him to his decision. Before his death, Glenn had written,

Tyler, What I'd started to write you about was not letting them sell out too much of the for the people and the by the people part of the oldtime United States way. . . . If not enough people believe in a way of life, it comes to an end and is gone.[24]

Tyler realizes, too, that his testimony would hurt Sue Ann and her children, that in any case he could not stop Chuck, and that, in the last analysis, it is "take the rap or turn state's evidence and save your shivering skin".[25] As he reaches his decision, Tyler hears Chuck's disloyal attack on him being broadcast over Chuck's illegally purchased radio station:

". . . although it's always possible that once in a while I have been deceived by the fair faces an' false smiles of some of those I trusted as Ceasar did Brutus . . . ah, there was the unkindnest cut of all, the stab in the back from a friend . . . I tell you-all here in this hall tonight that I have looked into the bottom of my heart an' I have found no guilt." [26]

Tyler, like Glenn, remains loyal to his ideal, even when the "machine" hypocritically turns on him. Tyler tells Ed James:

"We can't sell out on the people, but the trouble is that me, I'm just as much the people as you are or any other son of a bitch. If we want to straighten the people out we've got to start with number one, not that big wind . . . You know what I mean. I got to straighten myself out first, see." [27]

For Tyler, as for Glenn, there is defeat at the hands of the "machine", but for each there is the moral victory of being truer to the ideal than is the "machine" they serve.

3

The "machine" in *The Grand Design* (1949), the third volume of *District of Columbia*, is the New Deal administration of

---

[24] *Ibid.*, p. 230. Italics his.
[25] *Ibid.*, pp. 231-232.
[26] *Ibid.*, p. 240.
[27] *Ibid.*, p. 242.

Franklin D. Roosevelt. The book opens with the arrival in Washington, D.C., of the two characters who, like Glenn and Tyler Spotswood, travel the road of acceptance, disillusionment, and rejection. Millard Carroll, a successful businessman, takes a leave of absence to go to Washington to accept a job with the New Deal. There he is joined by Paul Graves, just back from Russia, who is hired as a subordinate official in Millard's agency in the Department of Agriculture. The large middle portion of the novel is primarily concerned with the efforts of these two sincere New Dealers to put into operation the idealistic goals which lured them to Washington. Millard Carroll struggles endlessly against red-tape; he attends parties which are notable only for their tedium; and he watches from the sidelines as the President and his spokesman, Judge Oppenheim, continually sabotage both the political hopes of Walker Watsom and the idealistic New Deal hopes of men like himself. At the same time, Paul Graves' life becomes a hectic tug-of-war with department officials, in which he has no help except from Millard Carroll. Paul also takes a series of trips into the "field" where he sees the effects of the New Deal on the people and gauges their attitudes toward it. Millard Carroll finally sees that he can no longer effectively execute his programs when the businessman Jerry Evans is given control of Millard's bureau and will permit no activities other than "business as usual". Millard resigns. Paul Graves, already bitter toward the "machine" on his own account, is further disgusted by Millard's forced resignation and makes his own plans to resign.

Unlike the first two volumes of the trilogy, where the point of view maintained was always that of a single protagonist, *The Grand Design* uses a shifting point of view, alternating between Paul Graves and Millard Carroll. This technique of shifting the viewpoint violates a minor structural unity within the trilogy, but it is necessary if the subject of the third novel is to be treated adequately because the "machine" in *The Grand Design* is too complex and operates on too many different levels to be seen entirely from the viewpoint of one character. Millard Carroll, whose job is just under cabinet rank, is the viewpoint for exploring the world of the "Boss", Judge Oppenheim, Walker Watson, and Jerry Evans. Paul Graves, through his trips into the field, is the medium for the exploration of the impact of the New Deal on the farmers and their reaction to it.

The central theme of individual and "machine" presented through Millard Carroll and Paul Graves is only incidentally touched by the communist infiltration theme, which really remains unintegrated, and by the isolationist theme – also unintegrated – which centers around Herb Spotswood, an ardent pacifist in *The Adventures of a Young Man* but an enthusiastic supporter of the war in *The Grand Design*. Herb Spotswood was probably intended to have some unifying effect on the trilogy since the first two books had centered each on one of his sons. His role in the third volume, however, is so small that his presence is of negligible value. The communist theme is of small use to *The Grand Design,* but it is interesting as a step in the thinking of Dos Passos. His first two novels had registered some hope that social improvement might come from the work of the extreme left. That hope was dead or dying in *Manhattan Transfer*, but nothing else had taken its place in the author's thinking. This temporary absence of a philosophical base is made clear in Jimmy Herf's leaving town to preserve his personal integrity; he rejects the system, but he knows no way to fight it or to change it, and his only alternative is flight. It is significant that in that book Dos Passos does not present the communist and anarchists as the possessors of valid solutions to the problems of society. In *U.S.A.* the Communist Party is indicted along with the rest of society, although Dos Passos deals sympathetically with a number of individuals associated with it. Then, in *The Adventures of a Young Man,* the Party becomes the major antagonist, and in *The Grand Design* Dos Passos heaps upon it the ultimate indignity in his repertoire: he fills it with homosexuals.

The only subordinate theme really integrated into the one concerning Millard and Paul is the one which relates the growth of New Deal bureaucracy. It shows the accumulation of almost unlimited power in the hands of few men and the widening gulf that separates the "Boss" and his few assistants from the American people. Indeed, it is this loss of contact which produces the situations resulting in the disillusionment of Millard and Paul. In this connection, it has been wisely written of Dos Passos:

He is an idealist who finds the human condition intolerable, who demands the millennium *now*. The imperfections he sees in the social organization arouse in him an instant, violent opposition to the status quo.[28]

The application of this truth to Dos Passos' changing attitude toward the Roosevelt administration – his attitude changed only when he felt he had detected a change in the attitude of the administration – is made plain in *The Theme is Freedom*: "It was somewhere during the years of the early New Deal that I rejoined the United States. I had seceded privately the night Sacco and Vanzetti were executed." [29] And again, he says,

On his first reelection in 1936 I had voted for him with enthusiasm. ... The New Deal in its early days had brought the country back to life. ... The financial regulators of the economy had been shifted from Wall Street to Washington without anybody's firing a shot.

But he adds,

The federal government became a storehause of power that dwarfed the fabled House of Morgan that had been the bogy of our youth. ... The trouble with immense political power of course is that no man is good enough to wield it. It's the fear of the loss of power that lets the evil in.[30]

Millard Carrol is used to illustrate Dos Passos' point of view in this respect. When he first arrives in Washington, he tells his wife, "I think we've come to the right place",[31] but before long he is echoing Dos Passos' fear of the "loophole for dictatorships" [32] by hoping that the "Boss" won't run for a third term. But Millard's primary concern is that of putting into practical operation the ideals of the New Deal. After he arrives in Washington, he works hard, but he soon begins to feel thwarted, maintaining that "instead of doing too much we aren't doing enough".[33] One of the

[28] R. T. Horchler, "Significant Tract for the Time", *The Commonweal*, LXIV (May 11, 1956), pp. 157-158.
[29] *The Theme is Freedom*, p. 103.
[30] *Ibid.*, pp. 161-162.
[31] *The Grand Design*, p. 41.
[32] *The Theme is Freedom*, p. 164.
[33] *The Grand Design*, p. 122.

many frustrations which Millard encounters is the constant entry of politics into every phase of government work. After he goes to see Walker Watson about departmental matters but has to listen to Walker's presidential aspirations instead, he goes back to his office where he tells Paul Graves, "Sometimes it looks as if we were here to provide window dressing." [34]

It is partially through Millard's association with Watson that the President's "virtually hypnotic" powers of persuasion are revealed. Dos Passos had documented those powers in an earlier work:

I remember . . . meeting . . . an American diplomaat I liked and admired for various reasons. He had an appointment at the White House. He was going to tell the President there had to be a change in policy toward the Spanish republic. . . . He was jumping up and down with determination. If the President disagreed he had his resignation in his pocket. I met the same gentleman a few days later at the same spot. No more talk of ending the blockade. No more talk of resignation. He and the President had agreed perfectly about everything. He had been talked around to the "larger view".[35]

This incident is used with devastating effect in *The Grand Design* when Walker Watson takes his presidential aspirations for a call at the White House:

"I've got to have the White House. He's got to make up his mind. I won't be treated like this. He can be the great leader of the American people without being President." [36]

After the dinner at the White House, Walker and his lady friend, Joe Powers, come to tell Millard the results of their talk:

"We must all help Walker take care of his health," Joe Powers rattled on brightly. "That was the last thing the President said. We must all do our best to keep him on his diet . . . and no speeches . . . a good rest out on a ranch in Montana . . . and particularly no speeches."

[34] *Ibid.*, p. 223.

[35] John Dos Passos, *State of the Nation* (Boston, Houghton-Mifflin Company, 1944), p. 149. Most of the facts and opinions given expression in *The Grand Design* were accumulated during a tour Dos Passos made of the United States in 1943 and 1944. His impressions were first published in a series of articles in various periodicals before being gathered into *State of the Nation*, and, finally, *The Grand Design*.

[36] *The Grand Design*, p. 226.

"He wants me to take better care of myself," said Walker with pride in his voice.

"He's got big plans for him at the convention," said Joe Powers. "He said he had to have Walker in good health for the convention." [37]

The irony in the insistence on "no speeches" is obvious enough, but when Walker goes to the convention and comes away with even less political stature than he had before, the "big plans" have been made quite clear.

The president's other voice is Judge Oppenheim who appears in person only twice but whose five telephone conversations equal almost anything Dos Passos had done in *U.S.A.* Structurally, the reason for Judge Oppenheim's inclusion in the novel is that he speaks in the persuasiveness and with the authority of the president to people who would have no earthly reason for conversations at the White House. Through him the power of Franklin D. Roosevelt is made to brood in the background and to exert pressure from above. The effect of each of the four conversations that Millard Carroll has with Judge Oppenheim is frustration and dissatisfaction. Once, for example, when Jerry Evans, the profiteering businessman, has been trying to work out his quasilegal plans by currying favor with Walker Watson, Ed James writes a column about their manipulations. Millard agrees wholeheartedly with the attack, especially as it pertains to Jerry Evans, and Millard plans not to attend a party which Jerry is giving for Walker. But Judge Oppenheim calls:

"Why, Judge Oppenheim," Millard heard the oil welling up in his own voice in a way he didn't much like. "How are you? I didn't know you were back in town. What kind of summer did you have?"

"Good enough, Millard, good enough. ... I hear you and Lucille are now old Maryland landowners. What a sweet child she is. Talking to her for a minute has been the only pleasant moment since we got back to take up the burdens of Nineveh ... tell her I said so." Millard found himself smiling as he listened attentively to the carefully pronounced sentences. "But Millard, what strange transmogrification has taken place in our friend the columnist? Has he had some kind of personal falling out with the great big rough diamond who is giving a party for the Watsons this evening? It is most embarrassing because

[37] *Ibid.*, p. 234.

the President is about to announce an important appointment which concerns him. I mean our rough southeastern diamond. . . ." [38]

And so on and on and on until it becomes a patriotic duty for Millard to attend the party.

The party turns out to be a climactic event in Millard Caroll's New Deal life, and, as so often happens in Dos Passos' novels dealing with men and "machines", the individual involved helplessly watches his fate being worked out for him by powers over which he has no control. Mike Gulick, formerly one of Glenn Spotswood's professors and now a spokesman for the New Deal, declaims at length upon how Millard Carroll, as head of the Economic Scarcities Commission, working under Walker Watson, can force foreign countries doing business with the United States to pay laborers fair wages, thus raising the standard of living in other parts of the world. While Millard is luxuriating in Mike's oratory and Walker Watson is suggesting hut-to-hut delivery of milk to every Negro in Africa, Jerry Evans comes in and announces that he has been appointed head of the War Procurement Board. The result of his appointment is that Walker Watson has been "passed over" again and that Millard's commission is under the jurisdiction of the materialist and sometime war profiteer, Jerry Evans, rather than under the idealist Walker Watson. The remainder of Millard's story is falling action. He has more and more trouble putting his desired programs into effect, even Walker Watson becomes a source of frustration, and, finally, there is nothing left for Millard to do but resign. The "machine" ejects him by applying pressure in the form of frustration. He has become incompatable with it because he continues to work for ideals which it has abandoned.

Paul Graves' hopes in the New Deal are expressed in his feeling that

The early settlers . . . had had some sort of a plan in their mind, a notion of how a free man ought to live on the earth. Now we'd lost that plan for America, lost it in press of business. The new Deal

[38] *Ibid.*, pp. 337-338. *See* also pp. 117-118, 216-217, 311-312 and 430-431.

was out to recapture that plan, an effort in that direction, better say, the beginning of an effort.[39]

Paul's own work for that "effort" meets with frustrations in the "field" as he becomes increasingly aware that when a "machine" tries to help, it must work with individuals rather than masses. Over and over again he finds that people do not know how to live with the help they receive from the government: one man cannot make the simplest adjustment on a cream separator, an elderly couple is afraid that the "Lectricity" might cause cancer, and a Negro family hasn't eaten the preserves prepared according to government specifications because "they're too purty".[40] A counterpoint is introduced in the person of the successful farmer, Hodgins, who, although he has privately resettled some of his own tenant farmers and made money for both them and himself, wants Paul's resettlement project to succeed. He tells Paul,

"There's an element in this country that can't help themselves. If the government can manage to show them the way to get on their own feet I'm all for it ... after all milk is milk and that's what we need to raise healthy kids the wide world over."

"Suppose our cooperative undercuts your prices?" asked the Reverend Green in his sharp voice.

Hodgins laughed quietly. "You try," he said. "Why, if you gave it away, I'll still have a better product and a market for it."

"Why?" asked Paul.

"Because everybody's business is nobody's business," said Hodgins dryly.[41]

On another occasion Paul explains his views to Nat Kubik, an independent, successful farmer:

"I'm in this because I think there's a valuable reservoir of people in this country who haven't gotten a break, farmers who live on submarginal farms, hillbillies, migrant laborers. Prosperity is an express that goes by mighty fast and makes very few stops and a lot of good people just don't catch the train for no fault of their own. So long as this government is willing to spend a few million dollars setting these people up in new farms and houses and in machinery to work with I'm willing to string along and see how it works." [42]

[39] *Ibid.*, p. 151.
[40] *Ibid.*, pp. 148-149.
[41] *Ibid.*, p. 157.
[42] *Ibid.*, p. 247.

Nat Kubik skeptically answers, ". . . the European war has done us farmers more good than all your New Deal experiments." [43] Finally Paul encounters John Hick, a wheat farmer with greater troubles of more varieties than any other man with whom Paul comes in contact. Hick explains why, despite his many problems, he doesn't want government aid: "Out in this country a wheat farmer's got to be a gamblin' man. We're just goddam . . . speculators . . . But I'm no bellyacher . . . I ain't runnin' to no government with my troubles." [44]

Paul's experiences with the individual farmers lead him to make a careful evaluation of his position between the "machine" and the people it is trying to help:

"Your relationship with people changes when you try to organize them into doing things. You have to kind of lower their consequence. First thing you know its your career instead of the work gets to be the important thing. I suppose that's how politicians are made. O God, don't let me turn into a politician.[45]

This feeling, coupled with his bitterness when Millard is forced to resign, prepares Paul for his disillusionment with the "machine" after Judge Oppenheim reveals the administration's attitude toward its own New Deal. In discussing Walker Watson, for example, the Judge says,

There had been every reason to fear that he would be more wedded than most to humanitarian schemes and commitments but since he had been in contact with the higher echelons, with the best military and strategic brains of Europe and Asia and America, he had made frequent sacrifices of his private views. It was impossible not to admire him for it.[46]

Paul hears the same type of thing from Walker Watson, who gives Paul an answer for Millard's desire to "install the Four Freedoms as we go along". Walker says, "Millard's a great feller. Tell him to look at this thing from the level of the leaders." [47] Paul's rejection

[43] *Ibid.*
[44] *Ibid.*, p. 264.
[45] *Ibid.*, p. 268.
[46] *Ibid.*, p. 431.
[47] *Ibid.*, p. 435. For Dos Passos' own views concerning the change in attitude of the Roosevelt administration, *see* also *State of the Nation*, pp. 181

of the administration for its abandonment of what he considers its highest goals is explicit in his statement to his wife:

"I been to see Walker Watson this afternoon. All he could talk about was the level of the leaders. I guess that's not for me. I guess we're the crowds along the sidewalk. It would be a relief in the navy . . . just lay back and take orders." [48]

the most striking thing about Paul Graves and Millard Carroll is that they are the first two of Dos Passos' heroes who enter into a major conflict with the "machine" and who withdraw from the conflict with their ideals and their personal lives undamaged. Millard Carroll can go back to his job and Paul Graves has both a commission in the navy and a farm waiting for him. Their success, if mere survival can be so designated, depends upon their withdrawing from the "machine" as soon as they realize that further conflict is useless. Glenn Spotswood refuses to withdraw; Tyler withdraws too late.

Another significant characteristic of both Paul Graves and Millard Carroll is that they are the first two important characters to have "roots" in the sense of belonging to the land and having established homes where there are people with whom they share a mutual sense of belonging. Concomitant with the sense of security they feel is their ability to survive the stresses imposed upon them without turning to some secondary source of courage. They are, in short, decent, middleclass American citizens – people whom Dos Passos had not included in any previous novel. This rather belated discovery of the middle class and middle-class values came to Dos Passos logically as a result of his rejection of the other two classes as the motivating power in society: one fattened men like Moorehouse and the other fattened men like Chuck Crawford. Dos Passos' acceptance of the middle class as synthesis necessitated a reorientation of some basic attitudes in subsequent novels.

---

and 222 and *The Theme is Freedom*, pp. 149 and 169-171. His views are largely those expressed by Millard Carroll and first agreed to by Walker Watson.

[48] *Ibid.*, p. 438.

4

Except for the four major characters in the trilogy – Glenn and
Tyler Spotswood, Paul Graves, and Millard Carroll – Dos Passos
is less interested in creating individuals or representatives of classes than in any previous novel. In *District of Columbia* his primary interest is in character types. Such important but subordinate characters as Herb Spotswood, Mike Gulick, and Walker
Watson are described not so much in terms of individual traits as
by generalized patterns of behavior. They become, not separate
people, but the "pacifist" turned "war-monger", the "liberal college professor", and the "obtuse politician". Dos Passos has found
characterization by type increasingly convenient and has used the
technique in all of his last four novels.

The structural unity of *District of Columbia* is not so obvious
as that of *U.S.A.*, but the three novels are well articulated as parts
of a whole. In the first place, there is chronological unity. *The
Adventures of a Young Man* picks up the thread of American
history where it had been dropped at the end of *The Big Money*
and carries the story forward into the thirties. *Number One* is
approximately parallel in time, but *The Grand Design* moves
forward again through the thirties and well into the Second World
War. Second, there is the thematic unity of the individual's conflict with the "machine". Third, there is the unity of the logical
progression in which Dos Passos postulates the ideals claimed by
the communist dictatorship of the proletariat in *The Adventures
of a Young Man* and the fascistic designs of Chuck Crawford in
Number One as thesis and antithesis. Benevolent bureaucracy
under the control of a president with almost dictatorial powers is
the synthesis presented in *The Grand Design*.

The internal structure of the books comprising *District of
Columbia* is not as integrated as is that of the three books of
U.S.A. Although more characters cross from one novel to the
others in the latter trilogy, the major characters do not do so to an
appreciable extent. With the exception of *The Grand Design,*
the novels are not as securely tied to time and place as are those
of *U.S.A.* The lyric prose passages which precede each chapter

of the three novels are at times more closely related to the theme than are the "Camera Eye" sections of *U.S.A.*, but with a few exceptions in *The Grand Design*, those in *District of Columbia* lack the intensely personal force of those in *U.S.A.* Nevertheless, these prose lyrics provide a sort of obligatto throughout *District of Columbia* to provide the author with a vehicle for stating explicitly portions of the theme that are also implicit in the narrative to which they are related.

Despite all the good things that can be said about it, *District of Columbia* is still much less imposing than *U.S.A.*; however, the author's fine hand in depicting scenes, images, and people remains visible. For example, at a party, Millard Carroll observes the following tableau:

Everybody was sitting on the terrace in the shallow garden shaded by ailanthus trees round a marble table that had a bowl of swamp magnolias on it. Their sweetness was heavy in the stagnant air saturated with the smell of sappy leaves and of women's perfume and coiling cigarette smoke. People hung balanced in the late afternoon stillness like fish in an aqarium.[49]

As is typical of Dos Passos' images, this one is clinched with a simile. Marice Gulick's character type is etched sharply when she tells Glenn Spotswood, "She thought the horrid old capitalist system was on its last legs. . . ." and later when she embarrasses him by telling her nine year old twins, "that their Uncle Sandy was mother's lover; but she said she believed in the most absolute frankness about those things, especially with the children." [50]

District of Columbia presents a large portion of the political history of the United States from approximately 1930 to the early forties. It traces the attractions of communism and reveals that doctrine's basic disregard for individual welfare and freedom, at least as it has been practiced. It also dramatizes the ease with which Americans can be led to follow a demagogue. These were the two paths out of the depression which Americans rejected. The political history of the New Deal as interpreted by Dos Passos in *The Grand Design* is his portrayal of the path actually

[49] *Ibid.*, p. 120.
[50] *Ibid.*, pp. 248-249.

taken by America. The third volume, too, contains the reminder that power corrupts to the love of power and that "machines" may turn against the ideals on which they are founded. The intense concern with the relation of the individual to the political machine looks forward to Dos Passos' significant post World War I non-fiction, *The Prospect Before Us* (1950), and the new type of protagonist in *The Grand Design* is indicative of a change in attitude which is more clearly revealed in *Chosen Country*. (1951).

IV. NOVELS OF THE FIFTIES AND *MID-CENTURY*

1

Dos Passos temporarily drops the theme of the individual and the "machine" in *Chosen Country* (1951), his first novel after *District of Columbia*. The previous novels had all been acts of negation, rejections of first one thing and then another – war, materialism, capitalism, communism, and so forth. *Chosen Country,* however, is a novel of acceptance; it is, in fact, downright sentimental. In it, Dos Passos goes back over ground that he had already covered at least four times – the post World War I period. This time, however, he makes the journey with a new kind of hero: Jay Pignatelli, who is a John Andrews without temper tantrums, a Jimmy Herf who knows what he wants and where to look for it, a Richard Savage who does not capitulate, a Glenn Spotswood who does not turn communist, a Tyler Spotswood who cannot be led astray by a demagogue. These comparisons are inevitable because Dos Passos exposes Jay Pignateli to experiences that each of the others goes through; in *Chosen Country* he is deliberately retelling the episodes, as well as a whole period of United States history, from an entirely new viewpoint. That viewpoint is one of sentimental patriotism which is vividly, if painfully, illustrated by Edward Everett Hale's "The Man Without a Country" (1863).

Dos Passos, in fact, makes extensive use of Hale's story. Jay Pignatelli, the illegitimate son of a wealthy corporation lawyer, frequently resembles himself to Philip Nolan, the central character in "The Man Without a Country", because he feels cut off from the world as a result of his illegitimacy. The structural pattern, then, is the search for belonging which, vague and lacking in direction at first, becomes increasingly specific and explicit throughout the novel. The search begins during a summer vacation from college when Jay visits a friend in Chicago where he meets Lulie Harrington. After Jay finishes his law course at Harvard, he joins the ambulance service and is sent to France where he has the same trouble with the Red Cross that Richard Savage experiences in *U.S.A.*, the primary difference being that at the end of the difficulty Jay goes into the army as a private instead of as a lieutenant. Taking his discharge overseas, Jay, like some of his predecessors, takes a job with the Middle East Relief in Constantinople. He encounters Russians, there is propaganda, and it is necessary for Jay to resign and return home via Teheran, Bagdad, and Beirut.[1] At home, Jay's cousin Nick Pignatelli persuades him to help with the defense of a Sacco-and-Vanzetti-like case. Jay gets one prisoner freed, but the communists gradually gain control of the defense committee, so Jay leaves the case. At this point Lulie Harrington asks him to handle a divorce case for her brother Zeke. Jay settles the case out of court, and he and Lulie fall in love; thus, Phoenix-like, one marriage rises from the ashes of another, and Jay and Lulie go valiantly into the future, hand in hand and declaiming lovely, patriotic speeches.

While the structural devices in *Chosen Country* have something in common with those of *U.S.A.*, they are sufficiently altered to allow the best presentation of the new theme. The cultural and biographical background for the characters in *Chosen Country* is related through three sections of *Prolegomena*. In these sections which occur in the first quarter of the book, the primary emphasis is on the parents and grandparents of Jay Pignatelli and Lulie Harrington. The ordinary "chapters" narrate the events of the lives of Jay and Lulie, with considerably more space devoted to Jay's life than to Lulie's. A third division, called "Footnotes", corresponds roughly to the "Biographies" in *U.S.A.* except that the biographies in the "Footnotes" are those of fictional char-

---

[1] The whole itinerary from Paris to Beirut is given more interestingly in *Orient Express* (1927).

acters, and the three fictional people thus treated are used in the narrative of Jay Pignatelli. The primary purpose of the "Footnotes" is to introduce new segments of Jay's life or to make his feelings clearer by means of comparison and contrast.

Lulie, who is a relatively static character, is slowly revealed in three chapters and one *Prolegomena* in the first two-thirds of the book. The really important thing about Lulie is that she be available and sufficiently explained by the time she is needed as a part of Jay's life. Jay's story is related through a series of events which inevitably lead him to find a person, a family, and a society to which he can belong. His initial insecurity is compounded primarily of his feelings of illegitimacy and his sense of rootlessness which is caused by the lack of an established home, friends, and family. Every time he feels insecure or reflects on the past, the major causes become tangled in his mind. Going back over his youth, for example, he thinks,

A Man Without A Country. Lord I cried over that story and Ishmael the wanderer in deserts and Cain, that birthmark on the forehead the mark of the accursed like Cain, like all history's bastards. . . .

Was it the bar sinister or the nearsighted eyes that made him always fumble the ball. . . . or the foreign speech or the lack of a home that made him so awkward, tonguetied, never saying the right word, never managing to do the accepted thing at the accepted time . . . He had few friends even now, though . . . he believed in friendship. Joe Newcomer was a prince, but even to Joe, Jay was the incomprehensible stranger who dropped in between trains.[2]

The Red Cross affair is the first significant episode in Jay's life after his graduation from Harvard. While he is in France with the Red Cross, Jay, like Richard Savage, gets into trouble with the organization while his really radical friends are promoted.[3] When he goes to see the Red Cross Major, also a Harvard man, about his trouble, his sense of isolation is reinforced:

It wasn't one Harvard man to another, not at all; the statement the major was groping for, that Jay could read, like print lit from behind, on his fat face, was that not every body who went to Harvard be-

---

[2] John Dos Passos, *Chosen Country* (Boston, Houghton Mifflin Company, 1951), pp. 26-27.

[3] *Ibid.*, pp. 337-338. *Cf. Nineteen Nineteen*, pp. 207 ff. The similarity between the two episodes is striking.

longed to Harvard really, some were illegitimate bastards with foreign names who had no social standing. . . . It took more than a few years residence in Cambridge to make a Harvard man.[4]

When he cannot force the army or the Red Cross to state the accusations, he contacts a member of his cousin's law firm and, seeing that he can do nothing about the situation, accepts the man's help in getting quietly enlisted in the army as a private. This episode is illustrative of two facets of Jay's character: first, his insecurity, and second, his ability to adapt himself to the "machine" when necessary. That Jay gets along well as an enlisted man and rises once to a mild heroism establishes that beneath his insecurity there is a core of strength.

The episodes built around Jay's work for the Middle East Relief organization, besides being Dos Passos' first fictional use of the trip recorded in *Orient Express*, teach Jay the dangers of communism and show the development of a social consciousness in him that eventually leads to his decision about his place in society. After being shocked by the suffering of the peasants in Constantinople, Jay is introduced to communism in Tiflis at a banquet at which the communist officers serve vast quantities of food while the peasants in the area are starving. The meal is followed by the sight of

. . . soldiers with bayonets on their rifles who were herding a group of ragged cringing men, bearded, filthy, their feet bound in rags, into a corner of the court. There rose from them the very stench of misery.

Jay is told that the men are being gathered up for a "Liquidation général" because they are "Counterrevolutionaries . . . Les capitalistes réactionnaires." He comments, "They don't look like capitalists." [5]

Leaving Tiflis enroute to Beirut with a distinct distaste for communism, Jay travels in the company of a medical student from Persia. It is this "Descendant of the Prophet" expounding the virtues of the political principles of Pan Islam that gives Jay a consciousness of what his part might be in America:

The law would give him a part to play in the life of his own country,

4 *Ibid.*, p. 339.
5 *Ibid.*, p. 376.

the way medicine gave the Descendant of the Prophet a part in Persia. He was tired of being a spectator in hell ... "To hell with the goregous East ... I'm an American, God damn it", he'd say to himself, "It's time I went home and went to work to grow up with the country." [6]

When Jay arrives in the United States, his cousin Nick Pignatelli, "Ceetizen of 'ooman race' " easily persuades him to accept the Sabatini case which has aroused the interests of the communists, who want a martyr and the big steel corporations, which want a conviction to prevent other strikes. The importance of the case to Jay is that it gives him a sense of participation in the affairs of his country, and, while it does not remove his sense of personal loneliness, it causes him to reflect more and more on his work as a lawyer, to the end that his practice becomes almost synonymous with citizenship for him. In conversation with a doctor, Jay indicates his feelings about his profession and his country:

"A lawyer is an officer of the court. Isn't it conceivable that a man might practice law as a public service?"
    "Public service," that's the biggest racket of the lot."
    "My father was an American by choice". ... "I feel the same way." [7]

Later Jay writes to a girl he had known in France, describing the case to her as a part of the struggle between the "barons of business" and the working men who were trying to organize unions as a part of "society's right to invent new forms". He perorates:

There are moments is every man's life when, just as if you happened to be on the street when someone was hurt in an accident, you have to do what you can to help. That's why I'm suddenly excited about being a lawyer. A lawyer is sort of a vulture who profits by other people's misfortunes, but at the same time he can be a defender of the civic processes that our liberties depend on.[8]

Jay saves the elder Sabatini, but the young man is convicted, and the communists force Jay out of the case before he can appeal the decision. Thus it is that he comes to terms with his own sense of inadequacy: "But if you do fail. ... Then admit failure." [9]

----

[6] *Ibid.*, p. 380.
[7] *Ibid.*, p. 389.
[8] *Ibid.*, p. 394.
[9] *Ibid.*, p. 446.

When Lulie calls Jay, then, to get his help in solving her brother's legal difficulties, he is considerably more mature than when she meets him the first time. Although he still feels a sense of personal loneliness which he reveals in another letter to the French girl, he has gained a sense of direction and a sense of participation in the life of his country; he has come to terms with himself. When Lulie accepts his proposal, his need for close human ties is satisfied. As they set out on their honeymoon, Jay, in a moment of tranquility, experiences an overflow of powerful feelings:

We've just scratched the surface of our country, it's still undiscovered; a newfound land ... Everything's to be done ... New means raw, unformed, disorganized. That's why we have to try and try again everytime we fail. ...

He wanted to be telling Lulie, in words that weren't flannel in the mouth, the yearning of a man who might have been a man without a country (Damn the United States: I never want to hear her name again) for the country of his choice that made him feel so proud and humble when he saw the striped flag fly.

He'd sound like a prig emitting these halfbaked notions out loud in front of the others. Not that he didn't love the others, he assured himself fervently; he did because they were Lulie's (and thy people shall be my people and thy gods my gods) ... You ungrateful bastard haven't you wanted a family more than anything in the world? But first Lulie, please; first Lulie and then the others.[10]

Jay, the descendant of Genoese emigrants, acquires a family and discovers the land for himself. Dos Passos plays upon the Genoese ancestry of Jay by bringing the couple to the East Coast to be married and then having them settle in a honeymoon cottage on a cove within sight of the waves and the rocks, planning to make "This wilderness our home." [11] It is enough to wring tears of joy from the D.A.R.

Aside from the new structural devices, the author's use of his various standard techniques for the presentation of theme requires little comment as regards *Chosen Country*. His uncanny knack of juxtaposition and irony are missing, and there are few striking scenes, few images fresh enough to arrest the reader's attention.

[10] *Ibid.*, pp. 465-466.
[11] *Ibid.*, p. 485.

Too many of the things that contain any measure of vitality are not new, but are borrowed by Dos Passos from previous works. The incident of the Red Cross majors is an example:

Fiat cars drawn up in a meadow full of buttercups at the end of a summer's noon beside a hunchbacked bridge. The drivers stood at attention and the Red Cross majors stood at attention and the gentleman and scholar [the founder of the service] out of another age had spoken his valedictory while at precisely fourteen o'clock the Boche as they were wont dropped a few shells on the bridge and the drivers stood quietly listening in the torn air and the gentleman and scholar had gone on, quiet monocle glistening in the sun, carefully picking his phrases for their New England pith, but suddenly the Red Cross majors were nowhere to be seen, only an occasional whipcord buttock protruding from the ditch beside the road. That was the end of gentlemen and scholars. . . .[12]

And practically everything which is described during Jay's travels between Paris and Beirut is lifted verbatim from *Orient Express*. The pity is that many fine passages from the earlier book are omitted. But despite its weaknesses, *Chosen Country* remains fairly readable; though a good deal weaker than any of the *District of Columbia* books, it nevertheless shows much greater skill than the novel which followed it.

2

Most Likely to Succeed (1954) is the story of Jed Morris, whose classmates had voted him that title. Jed, however, is a moral degenerate whose progress through the extremes of human decadence leaves little to imagine, and the title of the book becomes increasingly ironic. The "machine" is back again in this book; it is the Communist Party, and it accounts for Jed's destruction. Shortly after World War I, Jed arrives in New York from Morocco, where he has collected material for a play. He joins the Craftsman's Theatre, a "little theatre" which has three communists on the board of directors. He divorces his wife June and goes to live with Felicia Hardestie, a girl who has no more interest in com-

---

[12] *Ibid.*, pp. 338-339. *Cf. Nineteen Nineteen*, "Camera Eye (32)", p. 140.

munism than June had. When Jed's second play is produced by the group, it is a failure because the communists have insisted he take out much of the "good theatre" in order to make the play conform to the party line. Jed next goes to Hollywood where he takes a job as a screen writer. Felicia goes with him, but she rapidly becomes an alcoholic because of Jed's promiscuity. Jed is simultaneously drawn deeper and deeper into the Communist Party and deeper and deeper into the false world of Hollywood. When Felicia's second baby dies at birth, she leaves him and returns to New York. Jed becomes a minor official in the party and hires a girl named Marlowe to be his mistress and, incidentally, his housekeeper; then he falls in love with her. While he is still trying to convert her to communism, the local Party leaders tell Jed that he must choose between her and the Party. After great emotional turmoil, Jed sends Sam Faust to tell Marlowe that her services are no longer required and then succumbs to a well-earned heart attack.

Jed's rise to success in Hollywood and his increasing importance to the party is not marked by a corresponding moral degeneration as is Richard Savage's career in business. Savage is a dynamic character, having moral worth in the beginning of his career; Jed, on the other hand, from the very beginning is devoid of morals and is absolutely egocentric. His relation to the "machine" is virtually the antithesis of all the previous cases presented by Dos Passos, showing not the frustrations of an individual who works for certain ideals in spite of the "machine" – like Glenn Spotswood, for instance – but the perfect marriage of a morally impotent individual with a corrupt political organization.

Jed's character is established early in the story when he begins an affair with Marlowe on the way home from Morocco. He tells her,

"It's been a strenuous summer. First this damn play flopped . . . And then I kept waking up and finding myself in bed with some woman. There was a Spanish girl in Tlemoen who wore her hair a little like yours. She said she used camomile but she was only a common prostitute."

Then he introduces himself and asks her name:

"Jane Marlowe . . . Never mind my husband's name."

"I'll call you Marlowe, that's a golden name. Jane's too much like June. June's my wife's name."

"An adulterer, eh?"

"Consummate . . ." [13]

Jed's selfishness is nowhere better illustrated than in his reaction when Felicia tells him that she is pregnant:

"No woman can ever do this to me again." The words were on his lips when he woke up . . . It's not the expense, he wanted to explain to her . . . It's not that, he told himself, as he scraped the razor round the little point of his chin, it's that I'll be emotionally involved. He looked himself pityingly in the eyes. There was always that bit of a squint when he was upset. It would be too upsetting. It would take his mind off his work. Damn her he wouldn't let her upset him . . . She hasn't any right to upset me emotionally this way. He looked pityingly into the liquid brown of his eyes in the mirror.[14]

Jed's seduction by the Communist Party members of the board of director's of the Craftsman's Theater is very gradual. Sam Faust and Lew Golton, two of the communist board members, read his second play and come back with some suggestions:

Sam did all the talking. Looking everywhere except in Jed's face, he talked and talked. *Shall Be the Human Race* was a great document, it had all the possibilities of a smashing success both commercially and artistically . . . but there were loose ends that needed to be tied up. It was a question of a more disciplined distribution of ideas.

Lew Golton adds:

"Social-fascist implications . . . We want a play that the movement will stand squarely behind."

Jed's cheeks began to burn. "It damn well ought to stand behind it. It's the first time the revolution has been put on the stage . . . I mean in this country, of course," he added lamely.

Exactly. Sam made motions with his pudgy pale hands as if he were stroking velvet. That was why they wanted to smooth the kinks out. He had a friend who was thoroughly disciplined in Leninism, a man high up in the movement, a Marxist scholar. He'd consented to read it . . . His voice dropped to an awed whisper, like a man talking in a church. "V. F. Calvert has consented to come." [15]

[13] John Dos Passos, *Most Likely to Succeed* (New York, Prentice-Hall, Inc., 1954), p. 6.

[14] *Ibid.*, p. 118.

[15] *Ibid.*, pp. 98-99.

Jed insists on keeping some of the "ideologically immature" scenes, but in the process of the long discussions with the communists, he comes more and more under their spell. The failure of the play is explained by the director, Kenneth Magill, who blames the communists:

"And, dearie, they want it to fail ... They're doing everything they can to make it fail ... Because they hate me and because Jed wouldn't rewrite his second act to suit their ideas. He ried to please and the fell between two stools.[16]

But on the way to Hollywood, Jed is already spouting communist doctrine to Felicia:

"Feller, a man has to have a core of belief in him. Capitalism is dying of unbelief. That's why the bankers are climbing out of eighteenth story windows and poor Kenneth stuck his head in the gas oven. If he had believed in the future, if he'd believed in the working class he wouldn't have had to stick his head in that gas oven. ..." [17]

The core of belief in the future is made more explicit by Dos Passos in *The Theme is Freedom*:

Their movement offered men and women who subjected themselves to the discipline dedicated careers, the selfrighteous assurance that they were better than other men, and that sense of participation in history that takes the place of religion for the Marxist.[18]

It is this quasi-religious pull of communism that captures Jed so that he becomes an easy tool for the party.

The degree of his enslavement to the party may be measured by his relationship with Eli Soltair; before Jed becomes a communist, he describes Eli as his "best friend". Eli, who is worried about Jed's becoming a "real fellow traveler", argues with Jed about the party and its conspiratorial techniques:

"It's too damned efficient." Eli pushed his bloodshot eyes very close to Jed's face. He was so excited he spat a little when he talked. "It's all based on envy, hatred, and malice. Robespierre was efficient, at cutting off people's heads."

"He established the bourgeois revolution. Did he or did he not?"

16 *Ibid.*, p. 138.
17 *Ibid.*, p. 157.
18 John Dos Passos, *The Theme is Freedom* (New York, Dodd, Mead & Company, 1956), p. 40.

"Like hell he did," roared Eli. "He established Napoleon's dictatorship. Massacre, misery, and war followed," he added in a dramatic whisper, "by apathy and reaction." [19]

But Eli gets nowhere with Jed, and some time later when Eli petitions to join the communist dominated screenwriters association, Jed tells Sam Faust and Lew Golton, "Eli's not so much of a clown as he looks. He's a disruptionist. I vote to keep him out." And as Jed leaves the meeting, he worries because he knows that he may be suspect for having been a close friend of Eli's.[20] Jed also follows, without a murmur, the communist reversal of policy in the signing of non-aggression pacts with Germany. His only real difficulty is with Marlowe. "If only I could get you to see my way ... about the class struggle", he tells her. When she answers, "I guess you've never met a really loyal American before", he answers with a speech that sounds as if it had come from one of his own bad plays:

"All the women in my life have been pronounced reactionaries," he whispered in her ear. "I mean those I really loved," ..."We believe in different Americas," he went on whispering in her ear as they moved into the bedroom. "But love makes us one." [21]

At this point, Jed learns a new relation to the "machine" which he has given himself to; it is fear. When Jed awakens one morning and sees V. F. Calvert's car near his house, he encounters the full force of that fear:

His heart started to beat fast. No it couldn't be. What the hell would V. F. Calvert be doing out there that early? As Jed stood in the window gnawing on his cheeks he began to remember long ago the french window in a hotel room. Looking out over the sea. Little fragments of memory began to group themselves into a picture. That horrid Anna Glazunova panting in his ear and pointing with a crooked finger at the snubnosed freighter with the tiny patch of red astern ... "Cher ami it is finished." He couldn't remember just what had happened, only the terror and the Russian woman in her eveningdress lying sobbing on the bed. Silly, overwork. Pull yourself together, he told himself. ...[22]

[19] *Ibid.*, p. 193.
[20] *Ibid.*, p. 252.
[21] *Ibid.*, pp. 270-280.
[22] *Ibid.*, p. 305.

But when Jed goes outside to see what they want, and Calvert and Faust put him in the car without saying anything, Jed thinks they are taking him "for a ride". Instead they tell him he must choose between Marlowe and the Party, with a rather strong implication – "The discarded instrument is thrown out on the trash pile. Nobody hears much about him anymore" – that if he chooses Marlowe, the Party will destroy him in one way or another.[23] Jed, of course, chooses the Party and promptly has his heart attack.

Jed's relation to the motion picture industry, another kind of "machine", follows the well-worn groove of the young man who goes to Hollywood to make money so that he can return to New York and write great plays. When he first arrives, Jed hates Hollywood bitterly and detests the way the other writers toady to Milt Michelson, the boss. His immediate reaction is to "stick it out just to fool 'em" and then write a play to "expose" Hollywood, but he soon finds something "big about Milt" when Michelson compliments him and promises him a screen credit. The last stage is reached when Felicia's first child is born and Jed receives a personal note from Michelson. He reads the note over "a dozen times" before he goes to sleep. Jed's egotism and selfishness make him as much a captive of Hollywood as of the Communist Party.

From the standpoint of craftsmanship, the book is a great deal less well written than *Chosen Country*, which itself was characterized by a general weakening of technical powers. If *Most Likely to Succeed* is, as has been suggested, an attempt at satire of the *New Masses* or Greenwich Village communism, it is a failure and a weak joke. Actually this is probably not the case. After years of poking around in a philosophical wasteland, Dos Passos had finally discovered America in *Chosen Country*; once having made that discovery, he was in no mood to allow the communists – never really popular in his novels – to take it away from him, and having been well acquainted with the movement for years, he was frightened as were many other Americans during the fifties. This concern with the dangers of international communism is underscored in *The Great Days* (1958) and makes this con-

23 *Ibid.*, p. 309.

clusion all the more plausible. One thing is certain: Dos Passos had no love for his communist character, Jed Morris. Dos Passos had plainly lost his objectivity and his sense of humor, and the result was a novel which, Like Jed's play, fell between two stools. Fortunately, *The Great Days*, which followed it, is much closer to his second best efforts.

3

The "machine" in *The Great Days* is the "press" and other mass media which help to shape public opinion. This "machine" undermines the efforts of Roger Thurloe, the Secretary of Defense, who is the close friend of the major protagonist, Roland Lancaster. The effect of the "machine" on "Ro" Lancaster, himself, is just as disastrous, but his actual conflict with it takes place outside of the story. Only the results are visible. The "machine" ruins Thurloe by direct attack; it ruins Ro, a journalist, by not publishing his work and thus making him a "back number".

The story begins with Ro, a fifty-nine year old widower and "has been" journalist, trying to make a fresh start by going to Havana with Elsa, a young woman some thirty years younger than he. Elsa leads him on a wild career of drinking bouts, a night out with the "comparsas" or festival, a visit to the "non-objective" painter Pinillo, and a fruitless trip to a voodoo priest for charms for "girls who can't love". Ro gets a tip for a story, but the magazine he cables rejects the idea. Then his pocket is picked, and it becomes obvious that he and Elsa cannot establish a harmonious relationship. They return to Miami, and he sends her away, remaining in Miami, and saying, "Someday I might be needed."

But this is only half of Ro's story. The other half is presented through a series of reveries in which Ro remembers "the great days" when he and his wife Grace had been close friends of Roger Thurloe who became Secretary of Defense, of Mortimer Price who was also a government official, and of George Elbert Warner who, like Ro, was a famous journalist. During the reveries or "flashbacks", Ro recalls the wartime trips he had taken as a journalist: to England where he met H. G. Wells, to the Pacific theater, and to Europe where he learned to fear the Russians and where he had covered the Nuremburg trials. Finally he remembers his wife's death during an operation for cancer, Roger Thurloe's suicide, and the failure of his own book in which he had tried to point out what was necessary for America to do in the post-war world.

In this book, Dos Passos is once again back in the main stream of American history, picking up where he left off in *The Grand Design*. In this book, too, Dos Passos is once again the literary craftsman, employing his fine sense of balance and contrast so that the structure of the book is probably equal to that of any other single volume novel he has produced. First there is the frequent shift from Ro's shabby present to his more glamorous past and then back to the present, thus giving ample opportunity in a perfectly balanced allotment of space for the employment of contrast and juxtaposition which Dos Passos handles so well. Second, there is the progression both in the related events of the past and in the events of his present. His reveries begin with the memories of his greatest fame and his greatest personal happiness and end with his rejection by the American reading public and the death of his wife, while the narrative of his "present" begins again with a new woman and a new life and ends with an attempted suicide. Third, there is the careful arrangement of flashbacks with the other part of the narrative so that they complement each other; for example, Ro's attempted suicide is preceded by his recollection of his wife's death and is followed by his recollection of Roger Thurloe's suicide. And fourth, the two narrative streams are finally brought together when Ro goes to see Mortimer Price, hoping to borrow money from him. After he hears Mortimer descant on why Ro can no longer find a publisher, Ro cannot bring himself to ask Mortimer for money. Thus the man who explains the failure of the first life – Ro never catered to the public taste – also explains the failure of the second, and Ro knows before he goes to the cable office that his story will not be accepted.

Ro's career, which is paralleled and heightened by that of Roger Thurloe, is the career of a man who, after having allowed his private life to deteriorate through neglect while he worked for the "machine", suddenly finds his services no longer desired and himself rejected by it. Where Thurloe, a fairly obvious fictional Forrestal, ends his frustrations by suicide, Ro finds that he must go on living, endowed with fresh strength to endure, even though his attempt to start over fails.

The first part of Ro's story, which is largely based on *Tour of Duty* (1946), begins with Ro's trip to Florida with his wife, Grace. In Florida they visit the Warners, the Prices, and the Thurloes. Ro thinks, "What pretty wives we all had in those days and how well we all talked. We never seemed to get to the end of the things there were to talk about." [24] When World War II begins, Ro soon starts a series of trips to war areas as a correspondent. He undertakes his first trip to England with a "public mission for the magazine" and a "private mission for the Administration" which is imposed by Roger Thurloe who is now just under cabinet rank. Roger wants to know "how the outsiders feel".[25] It is the insistence of Roger that only through a reporter like Ro can he maintain contact with the people; this gives Ro a strong sense of identification with the "machine" and makes him conscious of being a part of great events in great days. When he returns from England, he reports to Roger Thurloe immediately, "Though I knew it would take some of the bloom off the articles I was getting up for the magazine." [26] When Ro tells Roger of H. G. Well's statement, "If you Americans can't find some way of carrying the burden of empire we are sunk, all of us, sunk!" [27] Roger reacts with an expression of dedication that becomes the driving force for both Roger and Ro as both become more and more concerned with the manner in which the war is waged and the peace that shall come out of it.

After Pearl Harbor, Ro worries because he is "not in uniform", but Roger tells him,

[24] John Dos Passos, *The Great Days* (New York, Sagamore Press Inc., 1958), p. 13.

[25] *Ibid.*, p. 41.

[26] *Ibid.*, p. 46.

[27] *Ibid.*, p. 50.

"Go on doing what you are doing. Tell the story, as much as it can be told, as it goes along. The American people are going to need some independent observers, Ro. . . . Take me in my job . . . if I cant get somebody to give me an appraisal from the outside I'll start believing it [propaganda] myself . . . Up there in the office I get everything through channels. I need some guys like you and Grace to keep me informed: How does it all look to the ordinary citizen? That's why I want you to keep out of uniform, Ro." [28]

Ro's second trip for his magazine and for Roger, who fears he is being "walled in", is to the Pacific area while the Americans are liberating the Philippines. Before Ro leaves, Roger reminds him of their common concern:

"Look here Ro, while we are fighting the war we ought to be laying the foundation for the kind of world we want to have after the peace. It's a subject I can't get anybody interested in in this town . . . but maybe more is being done than we realize . . . up from the grassroots, unconsciously . . . it's your business to find out." [29]

When Ro, who has already been in the Pacific for some time, prepares to go to the Philippines, he encounters Roger who has come because "I felt at least one of the men who helped make this decision had to go along." Roger asks Ro to "tell me everything about the Philippines", and adds, "I talk like I was your only reader." [30]

Exhibiting the same concern evinced by Millard Carroll in *The Grand Design*, Roger talks more and more about his concern for the condition of the world after the war. He tells Ro, "Whenever I run up against a considered plan there's a Muscovite somewhere behind it and their plan is to take us to pieces and dump us in Greasy Creek." [31] And it is Roger who urges Ro to do an article or book on "blueprint for the future" to give currency to the idea of the necessity of a planned course of action after the war. Roger also says he is trying to "hold off complete disintegration long enough for the country to come to its senses", and sends messages to Ro: "Tell Ro to write something that will convince people war

[28] *Ibid.*, pp. 69-70.
[29] *Ibid.*, p. 110.
[30] *Ibid.*, p. 145.
[31] *Ibid.*, p. 200.

isn't a baseball game. 'All right' the American public is saying: 'We won, let's all go home.' " [32]

Ro is caught up by Roger's concern for the condition of the post-war world, and when he finally goes to Europe to cover the Nuremburg trials, he tries to make a moral evaluation of America's conduct of the war in Europe and of the trials themselves. He finally begins to feel that even America has not come to Nuremburg with "clean hands". The divergence of Ro's view from the popular view is made clear in his argument with George Elbert Warner, who is careful to give the public the kind of reporting it desires. Warner asks,

"What are you going to tell the people back home?"

"The truth as best I can."

"You're going home to write a lot of goddam propaganda for the isolationists and the Facists and the America firsters. Do you know what I think we ought to do? After we've hung the bloody Nazis I think we ought to go home and hang the goddam isolationists."

"We've each got a right to our opinion."

"You shut up about your goddam opinions if you know what's good for you. You take it from me. Or I'll tell you right now what's going to happen. You'll wake up one of these mornings and find yourself a back number." [33]

When Ro returns to the United States he finds that he and Roger are already beginning to be "back numbers" despite the fact that Roger is appointed to "what was really the highest office in the cabinet". Roger is under almost constant attack from journalists and radio commentators like Wells Hartley who wants him to resign. Nevertheless, Roger reminds Ro of H. G. Wells' statement and urges Ro to keep on with his work on *Blue-Print for the Future*, reminding him of the Russian threat:

". . . if we let these people conquer the world it will mean the most brutal exploitation of the common man history has ever seen . . . We've got the power in our hands to thwart them. Just for a few years . . . We won't have it for long. All we need is the will to use it." [34]

But Roger is soon hounded out of office and commits suicide,

[32] *Ibid.*, p. 208.
[33] *Ibid.*, p. 236.
[34] *Ibid.*, p. 281.

and Ro's book, which Roger never has time to read, is a failure.
Ro summarizes his feelings:

All that Roger and I had left in common was deeply painful to both
of us. It was the failure of everything we had hoped for. It was his
defeat I shared with him as I read the sparse and pathetic details of
his end. His death seemed to seal that failure for us both forever. . . .[35]

While there had been war, there had been a need for them both,
for Roger to help make the decisions and for Ro to report to the
people; but now the war was over, and when Thurloe tried to
maintain strong defenses and Ro wrote about the danger from
the Communist "allies", they were attacked because of their unpopular ideas. Roger's final relations with the "machine" bring
him nothing but frustration and cause him to be hounded by the
press. His suicide is the last price exacted from him by the "machine" for his unpopular ideas. In Ro's capacity as a reporter, he
does not meet directly the same pressures that Roger meets, but
Ro's passage to oblivion is almost as swift. When he persists in
dealing with unpopular viewpoints or unpopular topics, he suddenly finds himself without a publisher – a "back number".

The second half of Ro's story reveals him in a new relation to
the "machine" and to life. He is making a desperate effort to get
back "in" although his feelings from the very start indicate that
he comes to it with a strong sense of defeat. Having a cup of
coffee with Elsa before their plane leaves for Havana, he imagines
the waitress's reaction to them: "Old enough to be her father",
and "a sick old fool doddering over a young woman." [36] Ro's
loneliness is demonstrated on the flight to Cuba. After a long
reverie in which he remembers his trip to Florida with his
wife, he thinks of Elsa and how he wants to tell her about his past,

To make her feel it's all part of me, everything I've ever been through,
everything I've told the world about, the voice inside his head is
saying, that's what I must make her feel.[37]

But Elsa is not interested in Ro's past. Once in Havana, when he
is trying to tell her about it, she takes the floor away from him

[35] *Ibid.*, p. 285.
[36] *Ibid.*, p. 8.
[37] *Ibid.*, p. 19.

to pour out her own story, and later she reveals her boredom by toying with the radio while he talks. After a long afternoon in Havana, during which they tour most of the bars, they go, at Elsa's insistence, to hear the music of Paco Cortes. Elsa is sexually excited by the music and by dancing with Paco Cortes. When she stumbles back to the table, she tells Ro, "Take me home. . . . Don't wait. Take me now." [38] As they return to their hotel, Ro thinks, "A goodtime Charley far past his prime, a drunken old goat dragged off to bed by a drunken whore." [39] On the following morning, the hopelessness of their relationship is made explicit in Elsa's asking a voodoo priest for charms "for girls who can't love".[40]

Ro deliberately faces the reality of his failure in his interior monologue on the morning of the second day:

"I should have known it was too late . . . It's not being broke. I've been broke before. It's not failing to make good with a woman, that's happened before . . . But in every love between man and woman there is a moment when a door in the heart opens. When your heart might have opened I didn't have the manhood to push in. Now it is too late. You caught cold you said out on the streets. I know what you meant . . . When I was a boy growing up somebody told me that if I could stand the unhappiness of adolescence everything else would be easy, but this is worse, Elsa, the frustation of defeat when you are a man grown and aged." [41]

His attempted suicide follows almost immediately, a climax to his frustrations; but he cannot go through with it, and tells himself, "You damn fool you don't want to die." [42] In desperation, Ro goes to see his old friend Mortimer Price, hoping to get a loan, but through Mortimer, he is reminded of his unpopularity at the end of what had been his "great days". Mortimer lectures him about his writing: "I don't understand why a man of your standing, Roland, lends himself to such distortions", and Ro sees on Mortimer's face only the "determination to be rid of an unwel-

---

[38] *Ibid.*, pp. 95-96.
[39] *Ibid.*, p. 97.
[40] *Ibid.*, p. 190.
[41] *Ibid.*, pp. 273-274.
[42] *Ibid.*, p. 276.

come visitor".[43] Leaving Mortimer without having asked for the loan, Ro stops at the cable office already knowing that his suggested article will not be accepted: "Mortimer is litmus paper. Mortimer's notions always did forebode the state of mind of the right thinkers." [44] The only thing left for Ro to do is to cash in their tickets for enough money to get Elsa and himself back to Miami where he sends her away on the bus. That part of his life, he knows, is finished. For the rest, for his journalistic career, it is the streaming crowds of people, of many separate individuals in the air terminal at Miami – "The lanky mechanic look. The cracker grin. The hick expression. My own people Ro is thinking; for better or worse it's to them I belong",[45] that give Ro the courage to hold on a little longer and perhaps to keep trying. He tells Elsa, "I'l wait here for a while ... Someday I might be needed." [46] Even though Ro's "fresh start" does not give him the kind of happiness he had hoped for, it does give him a sense of balance, a new perspective. He has confronted his own failure and come away from the encounter with the strength to endure.

The close harmony between structure and theme in *The Great Days* has already been discussed, but there are other indications in the novel that Dos Passos' technical mastery had not expired in *Most Likely to Succeed*. Once again his imagery is sharp and fresh and is sometimes heightened by strong contrasts as in the following:

He remembered Obispo as full of variegated overdressed people; tortoise shell and jet in jewellers' windows, embroidery work and alligator skins, lace mantillas, ... today the street seems long and empty with only the endless lines of cars grinding past. The window displays have a flyspecked look.[47]

The ability to establish a mood or a scene in an image of few words is again in evidence in such lines as "His life all at once appears visibly behind him like the road unreeling behind the rear window of a car" [48] and in these:

[43] *Ibid.*, p. 292.
[44] *Ibid.*, p. 295.
[45] *Ibid.*, p. 308.
[46] *Ibid.*, p. 312.
[47] *Ibid.*, p. 25.
[48] *Ibid.*, p. 28.

His sleep splits open as if an axe had split it. As the warm protective coverlet of his sleep falls away from him he lies miserably awake staring up into the dark with every throbbing nerve exposed. His head aches like a stone.[49]

Dos Passos has returned to the sharp, vivid image clinched with a simile. If *The Great Days* is less of a book than one of the volumes of either of the trilogies, it is because the more recent novel does not attempt as much, either in theme or in the devices used for the presentation of the theme, but what Dos Passos attempts in *The Great Days*, he does well. Whether he, like his character Ro Lancaster, could go back to his own great days by reemploying the scope and devices of *U.S.A.* in his first novel of the sixties, *Mid-century* (1961), remained to be seen.

4

In *Mid-century*, Dos Passos returns not only to an old form but also to an old theme, but to them he brings a new subject area and a new burst of intensity. It would be a mistake to speak of the book as *U.S.A* warmed over; rather, it is *U.S.A* continued, albeit with some decline in power and some little loss of verve. In it he is plainly returning to the structure that best suits his "natural history" of a society. The fictional narratives of *Mid-century* take up the American chronicle where *The Great Days* leaves off and include the following: Terry Bryant, a World War II veteran who is forced out of his job in a rubber plant by the union local because he attempts to make it give honest help to its members, and who is finally murdered by thugs hired by another union during a taxi company war; Frank Worthington, a labor leader who works his way up "from the ranks" and who finally compromises his ideals in order to remain in power; Jasper Milliron, a business executive and a hold-over from *Chosen Country* who loses out to financial manipulators in his effort to bring about a democratic decentralization and modernization program in the company he works for; Will Jenks, a young Korean War veteran who succeeds

[49] *Ibid.*, p. 98.

in breaking a taxi company monopoly in Duquesne but whose success is in danger at the end of the novel when it appears that the financial manipulators are "interested"; and Stan Goodspeed, a teenager who, in a very brief narrative, sets out on a blazing path across the country on the stolen credit cards of Jasper Milliron.

The "Biographies" are short, incisive life-summaries like those in *U.S.A.* and include such shapers of mid-century environment as Douglas MacArthur, Sigmund Freud, Samuel Goldwyn, Eleanor Roosevelt, Dr. J. R. Oppenheimer, Senator John McClellan, General William Dean, and labor leaders like Harry Bridges, John L. Lewis, Walter Reuther, Dave Beck, and Jimmy Hoffa. In *Mid-century* the "Newsreels" have been replaced by "Documentaries" which contain much the same sort of material as the former device, though with a greater emphasis on advertisements and materials taken from scientific writings as well as quotations from letters written to Senator McClellan's Select Committee. The "Camera Eye" sections are omitted, but there are four lyric prose passages written in the same style as the "Camera Eye". In *Mid-century* these passages are far less personal and less introspective than were the "Camera Eye" sections of *U.S.A.* Instead, they are calm, at times almost detached, contemplative musings on man and his relation to his institutions. There are two new devices in *Mid-century*. One is the "Investigator's Notes" sections which Dos Passos has said are the results of his conversations with some thirty workers concerning their complaints about union activities.[50] The other new device is the fictional narrative of Blackie Bowman which is presented in a series of reveries of Blackie Bowman, an old-time I. W. W. man who lies dying in a Veteran's Hospital. Blackie Bowman's memories, arranged in reverse chronology, are used to contrast with the narratives of the mid-century laborers. His memories represent the condition of labor in its early, poorly organized stage in contrast with the other narratives which show labor over-organized and too powerful. The author himself has suggested that he felt that in America the tendency has been to

[50] John Dos Passos in conversation with Dave Garroway, *Today*, N.B.C. Television Network, March 2, 1961.

allow "things" to get too bad and then to overcorrect or to let the "pendulum" swing too far in the opposite direction.[51]

There is little point in documenting the various conflicts of individual and "machine" in *Mid-century;* each struggle presented is a repetition of a type previously used, with only slight variations. Terry Bryant, for example, in his conflict with the labor union and his death in the taxi company war, resembles Glenn Spotswood entangled with the Communist Party and the Spanish Civil War. Frank Worthington is Richard Savage with better family morals. In his relation to the workers who elect him, he is much like the picture of Franklin D. Roosevelt in *The Grand Design* – a man who has "stopped listening". Jasper Milliron's story is a fairly close parallel to that of Charley Anderson except that Jasper remains sober enough to fight for what he thinks is right; thus, when he is forced out of the business, he lands on his feet with a great deal of money and with the woman he loves. Will Jenks appears in this novel to be a fairly successful Paul Graves gone into the taxi business. He fights the corrupt union and wins that battle, but the conflict with the financial manipulators is still pending at the end of the novel. The inconclusiveness of the stories of Will Jenks and of Stan Goodspeed and the placement of the latter's brief episode at the end of the volume, so reminiscent of the introduction of Charley Anderson at the end of *The 42nd Parallel,* bespeak the beginning of another trilogy.

Characterization, always Dos Passos' greatest weakness, is in *Mid-century* flatter than that in *U.S.A.* In his latest volume, Dos Passos seems to have stripped off almost every minor detail of his characters' lives, leaving only so much as pertains directly to his theme and leaving out much that might make them stand out more creditably as individuals. Blackie Bowman, through his occasionally rambling reminiscences, takes on a depth of character denied to the others in the book, and the whole of Stan Goodspeed's narrative, presented entirely in an interior monologue, shows how well Dos Passos can work in that form when he desires.

The general quality of craftsmanship and the handling of spe-

[51] *Ibid.*

cial techniques in *Mid-century* equals anything that Dos Passos has previously done. The episodes relating the handling of Terry Bryant's case before the state arbitration board is as fine a piece of satire as anything else Dos Passos has done in that line. The "Biographies' show, if anything, improvement. Speaking of Mac-Arthur and his first wife, he writes,

The union was shortlived. After the splendors of New York and Paris the lady is said to have found Manila, where MacArthur was appointed to his father's old post as American Commander, quite unamusing. It is admitted that the general lacked humor.[52]

And he adds later that "A proper brass hat doesn't know whether it's raining or sunshine until he's briefed by his staff. Like the queen bee he's fed on royal jelly." The "Biography" of Freud is more of an occasion to discuss psychoanalysis in general than an actual biography of Freud. Dos Passos writes:

> Man the misunderstood,
> incestuous, polymorphously perverse, narcist, masochist, sadist, exhibitionist, homosexual,
> has descended into neurosis,
> but through free association at twentyfive dollars an hour may seek redemption by total recall of that first prime talismanic wish – *In the beginning was the Word* –
> that he may rise again
> into the paradise of scientific psychoanalysis
> where Ego sits at the right hand of Superego in the sublimation of the Id,
> and transference is complete.[53]

His examples of the different types of psychoanalysts are devastating. He mentions Dr. X, for example, who "has a sharp nose for incompatibility between husband and wife, so that he is in great demand among the divorcing set" and who will "root the father image out of his female patients' dreams" and find the "housemaid little Johnny transferred to from Mama at the age of three". Finally he

well deduce the wellsprings of incompatibility between Mr and Mrs that gives them a thin time in bed.

⁵² John Dos Passos, *Mid-century* (Boston, Houghton Mifflin Company, 1961), p. 10.
⁵³ *Ibid.*, pp. 25-26.

They had better find transferences afresh. Dr. X sets up the specifications and sends them forth, insatiably cured,
to winnow the coctail parties for new mates.[54]

The use of contrast in the novel has already been suggested in the conterpoint of Blackie Bowman's story with the narratives of some of the other characters and with the "Investigator's Notes". Contrast is also implicit in the relation of the practices of labor unions to the purposes for which they were formed and the ideals on which they were founded. Juxtaposition, so adroitly handled in the "Newsreels" of *U.S.A.*, is also brought into play in the "Documentaries" of *Mid-century*. For example, there are such gems as the following:

Fallout can threaten more people than blast or heat in a nuclear attack.
So Pure and Gentle, Use it to Beauty-Bathe all the Costly Fragile Lingerie You Wear next to Your Skin [55]

LONG EARTHQUAKE WAVES *now available in actual sizes* [56]

US PLANS PAYLOAD TO LAND ON MOON It is a private world of rare and beautiful birds: [57]

But there is more in *Mid-century* than the reiteration of old themes and old forms, however technically well done. The thing that lifts this novel above the sometimes dead level of *The Great Days* and *Chosen Country* is that it has life and emotional impact; both the writer and the reader are involved again in a way that happened all too infrequently after *U.S.A.* Perhaps the best testimony is that after finishing *Mid-century*, the reader looks forward to the next volume in anticipation.

---

[54] *Ibid.*, pp. 27-28.
[55] *Ibid.*, p. 75. Italics his.
[56] *Ibid.*, p. 191. Italics his.
[57] *Ibid.*, p. 487.

V. SOME CONCLUSIONS

John Dos Passos is a better biographer than a poet, a better poet than historian, a better historian than novelist. He chose to write novels; therefore his best novels are those which make most use of his other talents, which are considerable. It is this set of circumstances which makes *Manhattan Transfer, U.S.A.*, and *Mid-century* his best works. It is this set of circumstances that makes his best non-fiction a great deal better than his second-best fiction and inferior to his best fiction only because of the "Biographies" in the fiction. It is this set of circumstances that makes Dos Passos' plan for the great American chronicle – a social, political, economic history in novel form – so suitable to him as a novelist. And he has carried that chronicle from the turn of the century to the present time. Listed in order, the novels of the chronicle are as follows: *The 42nd Parallel, Nineteen Nineteen, The Big Money, The Adventures of a Young Man, Number One, The Grand Design, The Great Days*, and *Mid-century*. Overlapping with some of these and broadening the coverage of the periods are *Manhattan Transfer* which cuts across the whole of *U.S.A., Chosen Country*, which overlaps the two trilogies through the twenties and thirties, and *Most Likely to Succeed*, which is roughly concurrent with the whole of *District of Columbia*, the first two volumes of which are, incidentally, also concurrent. The first three novels are not listed because it seems probable that the concept of the chronicle had not been formulated at the time they were written; they do, of course, fall within the time covered by the chronicle.

Such a chronicle is, of itself, a major undertaking and a significant contribution to the social sciences as well as to art, but Dos Passos is not doing bare reporting, mere cataloguing of facts; he sees a recurring pattern in American society and in her social institutions, and he has sought to make this pattern clear in most of his novels. Basically, his indictment of the social institution – the "machine" – is that, regardless of what dedicated purpose it is designed to fulfill or on what pure ideals it is founded, the "machine" eventually ceases to function for the fulfillment of the original purpose or for the preservation of those ideals and gradually begins to function for the preservation of itself. The active ingredient in the process by which this change takes place is man's desire for power. In order to accomplish certain worthy ends, society creates an institution or a "machine", which, if it is to function properly, must be delegated certain power or authority: the people must give up some of their individual liberties to it. Power corrupts; once the "machine" had grown strong enough to do so, it sets about insuring its own preservation by acquiring even more power, paying scant heed to its original purposes or ideals. At times, indeed, the "machine" may even attack the very things it was designed to protect or to foster. The result of the change in the "machine" is the material success and moral corruption of those who function as a part of it and the destruction of those who oppose it. The destruction wrought by the "machine" may be either moral, economic, social, or physical.

Dos Passos suggests a number of patterns of relationship between the individual and the "machine", and these patterns determine the structure of the novels. First, there are those individuals who are ignorant of the existence of the "machine" or who, at least, have only the slightest notion of the significance of it in their lives. These people, like Chrisfield (*Three Soldiers*) and Joe Williams (*U.S.A.*), are gradually destroyed by the forces which they do not understand and therefore cannot deal with.

Among the second group, those who accept the "machine" and whatever changes it may undergo, there are those like James Merivale (*Manhattan Transfer*) and J. Ward Moorehouse (*U.S.A.*) who accept the "machine" unconsciously, who, without making a deliberate moral choice about the "machine", automatically assume it to be a proper part of their existence. These people are either unconscious even of the necessity for making a moral choice because they believe, basically, that whatever is, is right, or they are so thoroughly conditioned to the machine that its corruption is not seriously repellant to them. For such characters there is usually the pattern of economic and social success accompanied by a corresponding spiritual decay.

Among those who consciously choose to abide by the dictates of the "machine" in order to attain some end, some are granted a momentary, apparent success followed by a very obvious total failure as are Fuselli (*Three Soldiers*) and Charley Anderson (*U.S.A.*). Others, more intelligent or more skillfull in their particular professions, manage to gain a real economic and social advantage, but it is for this group, including such characters as Richard Savage (*U.S.A.*) and Jed Morris (*Most Likely to Succeed*), that Dos Passos reserves the greatest moral decadence. Having sufficient mentality to make the moral choice, having deliberately chosen the morally wrong, and having deliberately prostituted their talents and intellect in the service of it, they sink to the moral level of absolute zero.

For another group there is a pattern of admiration for and acceptance of the "machine", followed by a gradual disillusionment as it becomes obvious that the "machine" is not really what it seems or that it no longer lives up to its purpose and ideal. The final stage is rejection of the "machine". Some characters, like Glenn Spotswood (*Adventures of a Young Man*) and Terry Bryant (*Mid-century*) attempt to force the "machine" to live up to its purpose and its ideals. In the process of their struggle, they generally follow a pattern which is the reverse of that followed by men like Richard Savage and Jed Morris; that is to say that while Glenn Spotswood and Terry Bryant are destroyed socially, economically, and eventually, physically, there is a corresponding spiritual growth so that their defeat by the "machine" results in a moral victory for them. Some who come to reject the "machine" do not enter a conflict with it directly; they merely withdraw from it. These are like Jimmy Herf (*Manhattan Transfer*) and Paul Graves (*The Grand Design*) who find that since they cannot change the "machine", their only choice is to withdraw with honor rather than to remain and be corrupted.

Among the variants from the general patterns of relationships are those who attempt to escape the "machine" like Nan (*Streets of Night*) and Eveline (U.S.A.) but who turn to something as false as that from which they flee. There are also the parasites on the successful, such as Eleanor (*U.S.A.*) who follow a pattern such as that followed by Moorehouse.

Perhaps the one major criticism that might be made of all this about men and "machines" is that what happens in the novels seems to happen, not because men are as they are, but because "machines" are as they are. This weakness is obviously related both to Dos Passos' primary difficulty in creating complex, believable people for his stories and to his particular methods of organizing his stories into the historical-social-cultural background. A singular thematic problem arises from his thus placing the blame on the "machine" rather than on the weakness of man; it is that Dos Passos will never, without raising up an epic hero, be able to show man triumphant over his "machines". The best that he has been able to do thus far is a successful withdrawal for a few heroes. According to the analysis Dos Passos makes in his non-fiction *The Prospect Before Us* (1950), the only possible way for man to control his "machines" is to eliminate as many of them as possible and then to work actively and intelligently in all that remain so that they will be forced to continue responsive to the will of the people they affect. The human experience does not at the present time suggest the likelihood of such a solution being attained.

But most of the flaws in the writing of Dos Passos are the result of the enormity of the task he has undertaken, and it is this task that holds the reader's attention. In his yet unpublished novels there will doubtless be biographies of such men as John F. Kennedy, Lee Harvey Oswald, Lyndon B. Johnson, Martin Luther King, and Barry Goldwater. He has not yet touched on the civil rights movement, the Ku Klux Klan, the John Birch Society, nor the controversial procedures of the House Un-American Activities Committee. He has not yet touched with his acid, façade-dissolving humor the précieux agony of the Beat Generation nor the monstrous absurdity of the topless bathing suit. Those who have learned what may be expected from Dos Passos' investigations of both the depths and the shallows of American society await his diagnosis.

BIBLIOGRAPHY

PRIMARY SOURCES – A CHRONOLOGICAL LISTING

Dos Passos, John, *One Man's Initiation-1917* (London, George Allen & Unwin Ltd., 1920).

——, *Three Soldiers* (New York, The Modern Library, 1932). First published by George H. Doran Company in 1921.

——, *A Pushcart at the Curb* (New York, George H. Doran Company, 1922).

——, *Rosinante to the Road Again* (New York, George H. Doran Company, 1922).

——, *Streets of Night* (New York, George H. Doran Company, 1923).

——, *Manhattan Transfer* (Boston, Houghton Mifflin Company, 1925).

——, *The Garbage Man, A Parade with Shouting* (New York, Harper & Brothers, 1926).

——, *Facing the Chair; Story of the Americanization of Two Foreignborn Workmen* (Boston, Sacco-Vanzetti Defense Committee, 1927).

——, *Orient Express* (New York, Harper & Brothers, 1927).

——, *In All Countries* (New York, Harcourt, Brace & Company, 1934).

——, *Three Plays* (New York, Harcourt, Brace & Company, 1934). Contains "Airways, Inc.", "Fortune Heights", and a revised version of "The Garbage Man".

——, *U.S.A.* (New York, The Modern Library, 1937). Contains *The 42nd Parallel* (1930); *Nineteen Nineteen* (1932) and *The Big Money* (1936).

——, *Journeys Between Wars* (New York, Harcourt, Brace & Company, 1938).

——, *The Ground We Stand On; Some Examples from the History of A Political Creed* (New York, Harcourt, Brace & Company, 1941).

——, *State of the Nation* (Boston, Houghton Mifflin Company, 1944).

——, *First Encounter* (New York, Philosophical Library, 1945). A reprint of *One Man's Initiation-1917*.

——, *Tour of Duty* (Boston, Houghton Mifflin Company, 1946).

——, *District of Columbia* (Boston, Houghton Mifflin Company, 1952). Contains *Adventures of a Young Man* (1939), *Number One* (1943), and *The Grand Design* (1949).

——, *The Prospect Before Us* (Boston, Houghton Mifflin Company, 1950).

——, *Chosen Country* (Boston, Houghton Mifflin Company, 1951).

——, *The Head and Heart of Thomas Jefferson* (Garden City, New York, Doubleday & Company, 1954).

——, *Most Likely to Succeed* (New York, Prentice-Hall, Inc., 1954).

——, *The Theme is Freedom* (New York, Dodd, Mead & Company, 1956).

——, *The Men Who Made the Nation* (Garden City, New York, Doubleday & Company, Inc., 1957).

——, *The Great Days* (New York, Sagamore Press, Inc., 1958).

——, *Prospects of a Golden Age* (Englewood Cliffs, New Jersey, Prentice-Hall, Inc., 1959).

——, *Mid-century* (Boston, Houghton Mifflin Company, 1961).

——, *Mr. Wilson's War* (Garden City, New York, Doubleday & Company, Inc., 1962).

——, *Brazil on the Move* (Garden City, New York, Doubleday & Company, Inc., 1963).

——, *Occasions and Protests* (Chicago, Henry Regnery Co., 1964).

Dos Passos, John, "July", *The Transatlantic Review*, II (August, 1924), 154-179.

——, "Back to Red Hysteria", *The New Republic*, LXIII (July 1, 1930), 168-169.

——, "A Communication", *The New Republic*, LXIII (August 13, 1930), 371-372.

——, "The Business of a Novelist", *The New Republic*, LXXVIII (April 4, 1934), 220.

——, "Migratory Worker", *Partisan Review*, IV (January, 1938), 16-20.

——, "The Situation in American Writing", *Partisan Review*, VI (Summer, 1939), 26-27.

——, "Reminiscences of a Middle-Class Radical", *National Review*, I (January 18, 1956), 9-11.

——, "What Union Members Have Been Writing Senator McClellan", Reader's Digest, LXXIII (September, 1958), 25-32.

SECONDARY SOURCES

Beard, Charles A., and Mary R., *The Rise of American Civilization* (New York, The Macmillan Company, 1930).

Eastman, Max, and others, *John Dos Passos, an Appreciation* (New York, Prentice-Hall, 1954).

Feied, F. J., *No Pie in the Sky* (New York, Citadel Press, 1964).

Gelfant, Blanche Housman, *The American City Novel* (Norman, Oklahoma, University of Oklahoma Press, 1954).

Hoffman, Frederick J., *The Modern Novel in America 1900-1950* (Chicago, Henry Regnery Company, 1951).

Lerner, Max, *Ideas Are Weapons; The History and Uses of Ideas* (New York, Books, Inc., Viking Press, 1943).

Lewis, Sinclair, *John Dos Passos' Manhattan Transfer* (New York, Harper & Brothers, 1926).

Morison, Samuel Eliot and Henry Steele Commager, *The Growth of the*

American Republic, 2 vols. (New York, Oxford University Press, 1950).

Potter, Jack, *A Bibliography of John Dos Passos* (Chicago, Normandie House, 1950).

Rideout, Walter B., *The Radical Novel in the United States 1900-1954* (Cambridge, Harvard University Press, 1956).

Vernadsky, George, *A History of Russia* (New Haven, Yale University Press, 1944).

Wrenn, J. H., *John Dos Passos* (New York, Twayne, 1961).

Bernardin, Charles W., "John Dos Passos' Harvard Years", *The New England Quarterly*, XXVII (March, 1954), 3-26.

Cowley, Malcolm, "Afterthoughts on Dos Passos", *The New Republic*, LXXXVIII (September 9, 1936), 134.

——, "Dos Passos and His Critics", *New Republic*, CXX (February 28, 1949), 21-23.

Farrell, James T., "Dos Passos and the Critics", *The American Mercury*, XLVII (August, 1939), 489-494.

——, "How Should We Rate Dos Passos?", *New Republic*, CXXXVIII (April 28, 1958), 17-18.

Frohock, W. M., "John Dos Passos of Time and Frustration", 2 parts, *Southwest Review*, XXXIII (Winter and Spring, 1948), 71-80 and 170-179.

Geismar, Maxwell, "Young Sinclair Lewis and Old Dos Passos", *The American Mercury*, LVI (May, 1943), 624-628.

Hicks, Granville, "Dos Passos – The Fruits of Disillusionment", *New Republic*, CXXXI (September 27, 1954), 17-18.

——, "John Dos Passos", *Bookman*, LXXV (April, 1932), 32-42.

——, "The Politics of John Dos Passos", *The Antioch Review*, X (March, 1950), 85-98.

Horchler, R. T., "Significant Tract for the Time", *The Commonweal*, LXIV (May 11, 1956), 156-158.

Howe, Irving, "John Dos Passos: The Loss of Passion", *Tomorrow*, VII (March, 1949), 54-57.

Kallich, Martin, "John Dos Passos: Liberty and the Father Image", *The Antioch Review*, X (March, 1950), 99-106.

Landsberg, Melvin, "Author Dos Passos", *The New York Times Magazine*. July 7, 1957, p. 2.

Lydenberg, John, "Dos Passos and the Ruined Words", *The Pacific Spectator*, V (Summer, 1951), 316-327.

Sanders, David, "The 'Anarchism' of John Dos Passos", *The South Atlantic Quarterly*, LX (Winter, 1961), 44-55.

INDEX